# MY
# MIRACLE
# CURE

# MY MIRACLE CURE

*An extraordinary story of hope,
healing and the power of faith*

## MARION CARROLL

### with John Scally

BLACK & WHITE PUBLISHING

First published 2020
by Black & White Publishing Ltd
Nautical House, 104 Commercial Street
Edinburgh, EH6 6NF

1 3 5 7 9 10 8 6 4 2    20 21 22 23

ISBN: 978 1 78530 293 0

A CIP catalogue record for this book is available from the British Library.

Typeset by Iolaire, Newtonmore
Printed and bound by CPI Group (UK) Ltd, Croydon, CR0 4YY

'Everyone I have observed listening to
Marion's story goes away with a feelgood factor.'

– JOHN HYNES, President of the Knock Shrine Society

*Thanks to all who have helped me on my journey.*

# Contents

# 1

# At Death's Door

*'The fruit of letting go is birth.'*

— MEISTER ECKHART

*Sunday, 3rd of September 1989, 6.12 a.m.*
The only sound was the ticking of the clock and my husband's steady breath.

I was scared.

No.

Correction.

I was very scared.

I was tired.

I was unprepared for dying.

But that was what was facing me.

The only question was: would it be weeks or months?

Maybe if God was very good to me, I might get a few more years.

I would gladly take that even if inevitably I would be just a shell of my former self.

The image of Jesus on the cross had just taken on a new significance for me.

I stared at my hand in my lap, clasped so tightly the knuckles had turned a translucent white.

But I felt the shock in my blood, actually felt it pumping and churning inside me.

I had never known anything like it.

I just wanted things back the way they used to be.

The harsh reality of my battered body stung.

It was as though I had been cut; the knife having gone so deep that the wound was not yet painful, it produced merely shock.

It seemed to me, after that awareness, that the world was thoroughly altered.

It was not something I could explain adequately, why it was that everything was folly.

So much of what excited people in normal life suddenly seemed wholly and disturbingly petty. An almost nostalgic pang of memory came over me as I remembered all my happy days with my family.

The day I married Jimmy.

The birth of my two lovely children, Cora and Anthony.

I could not remember time looping in on itself in such a manner before, when life had been measured out in minutes rather than in hours. A sadness so deep that no tears could come.

It was Sunday, but days of the week didn't really matter to me anymore.

I thought about the illness that would claim my life. Six months later maybe?

Jimmy's words were full of positivity about the prognosis, but the uncharacteristic hesitancy in his voice told another story.

Earlier that week, my beloved husband glanced around him with an expression of faint alarm. He raised his eyes and I saw it all in an instant over his face. Love. Family. Responsibility. All to be lost? These things Jimmy understood instinctively. He never gave them voice, not even within the privacy of his thoughts.

Last time I was in the hospital, a nurse with blonde hair peered anxiously at me as I walked unsteadily down the corridor. She smiled, faintly uncomfortable with the slight strain of sociability, as I was drenched by reminiscences that seemed to have no regard for circumstances or place.

### 6.30 a.m.

My mind crowded, as though there were a critical fact teasing me at the periphery of my brain, a detail I ought to be thinking about, a memory I ought to be seizing, a solution to a problem that seemed just beyond my grasp.

Something unusual was happening this day.

But what was it?

Then it came to me.

Today was the day I was going to Knock.

Did I want to go?

No.

Could I come up with a good excuse not to go?

No.

Not really.

Not one Jimmy would accept anyway.

This was a man capable of the most subtle investigation of aspects of the human condition, which philosophy and theology have customarily claimed as their proper territory.

I felt I had come face to face with what scholastics call 'the ground of being'. Memories pricked at me, nagged at me: Jimmy placing the ring on my finger on our wedding day, the priest intoning the sentences with gravitas, the birth of my children. I was amazed at how intensely visceral the fear of my own death was. I frowned steadily, my brows knitted like a child over their homework – frustrated – that area in myself had become so powerful that it threatened to swallow everything else. These were my Stations of the Cross.

*A Few Hours Earlier*

That night I stayed awake because of this sudden separation from the world of pure dreams, where all things are made of enchantment, and where there is no suffering. I heard every crack on the corridor, every microscopic night-time noise on the hall, juxtaposed on to the distant sound of light traffic along the road in Athlone. I only fell asleep just before dawn when the birds, like an out-of-tune choir, set up a shrill contest of noise, a chorus that drowned out the gentle vibration of traffic and every other sound, and blanked out every danger.

My dream.

No.

My nightmare.

I saw my own funeral.

It will live with me for ever – looking down on a gathering for an occasion almost unbearably sad: a centre of my life gone. I was near to tears and, in my heart, there was something stirring, a sense of outrage, a feeling of total despair. I could not bring myself to think of myself in the past tense, but I had seen the evidence of the previous night as I lay in my coffin. I seemed so calm as I smiled and held my rosary beads in my hand. I hoped fervently my soul had been set free from its anguish and that I would find peace at last in a higher, more perfect world.

There was no strain anymore, and the features of my face were calm, now that I had been released from the struggle for breath.

As I journeyed in the coffin to the graveyard after my funeral, in a scene sculpted in sadness, the emptiness I felt pervaded everything. I found I couldn't put my thoughts away and I began to understand how I would miss my family. Like a hidden grieving that rises to grab the heart, my soul was ambushed with old emotions, and my lips began to tremble, and for a brief instant I was swept into the current of all that I had lost.

The worst thing about my illness is that nobody else can see it or feel it. The energy is just drained from my body and mind. To other people, I look okay from a distance but the whole time I just want to sleep and then, when I awaken, I am feeling like I never slept at all and need to sleep again. It is like a hangover after a hard night's drinking, but not a drop of alcohol has been consumed at all. And that is on one of my best days now.

For months, maybe even years, I have really felt that my body has taken a severe hammering. The fact that I have no energy much now to go walking and keeping in shape – and also the fact I have no control really anymore of what I can do – is really scaring me. It is not being in control of my mind and my physical body that has seriously ground my life to a shuddering halt, but through all of this I had always to remain positive in my mind and in my spirit.

But now that resolution has become as broken as my body.

I woke from my nightmare.

Yet as I travelled in my thoughts, I was thankful.

I turned to look at Jimmy in his sleep.

I knew that, despite the tragic circumstances of my forthcoming death, my life was greatly enriched by such a man. Nobody did more than him to make me feel loved so well.

My mind flashed back to a day, a day so wet even the puddles had waves in them, when Jimmy entered my life for the first time. Legend had it that when he shook your hand it was shook for ever. I recalled the immediate authority that draped itself over his face that day.

Then there was his voice that I would hear no more. I remembered how quickly I learned not just to listen to the words he had used, but also to the tones in which I could distinguish delicacy, irony and compassion.

I wondered why God could allow the premature sacrifice of such wealth.

Life is full of riddles that only the dead can answer.

Soon I would be one of them.

## High Noon: the Knock Shrine Basilica

For one hundred and forty years, Knock has been the one fixed point in a fast-changing age. Those years have not been without their troubles but, even when the storm clouds gathered, the people's place of pilgrimage has not withered before their blast and a greener, better, stronger movement lay in the sunshine when the tempest was past.

Our economic system values measurable outcomes, but what is deepest about us transcends what can be said and outstrips what can be analysed. It is not given to us to peer into the mysteries of the future, but we can safely predict that in the coming one hundred and forty years, the story of Knock will continue to reach to something profound within us. For what, we may not always be sure. Except that there are moments when we know that there is more to life – and to us – than the grim and grasping existence of seeking and striving and succeeding.

There are moments of wonder, hope and grace that give us hints of ecstasy and lift us out of ourselves. They are, in Yeats's phrase, 'the soul's monuments of its own magnificence'. These moments take us to the heart of the deep mystery of being a person, the subterranean stirrings of the spirit, the rapid rhythms of the human heart. They have to do with remembering who we are, enlarging our perspective, seeing ourselves whole.

In his visit to Ireland in August 2018, Pope Francis reminded us that in our modern world we need to pray more than ever. But in our busy, often frenetic, lives today is there still time and space for prayer?

I tried to pray but I couldn't.

My mind was racing.

I thought of Bette Midler.

I thought about how she opened her famous song with lines about living in the shadows before asking whether you ever knew you were my hero.

Jimmy is the wind beneath my wings.

I wished he could say the same about me.

Soon I would be no help to him.

Here I was, on a stretcher, and soon there would be no more wind beneath my wings.

Jimmy was a hero in the true sense of the term because, when he helped me, *do lioigh an laoch san uile dhuine* ('the hero in all of us was exulted'). From the dawn of time, identification with heroes has been an integral part of the human condition. Great people have always grabbed the imagination of the young of all ages as they fantasise about emulating the glorious feats of their heroes. Thanks in no small part to television, heroes occupy an even larger part of the imagination today than in earlier generations.

William Butler Yeats exhorted people go to their graves empty, having not wasted a moment of their lives. Jimmy need have no worries on that score. It is given to few mortals to be eternally remembered after their stint in this vale of tears is over, even fewer as a consequence of their achievements for helping a woman like me. With the passing years, Jimmy's name would have an even stronger evocative power: it would be a chant, an invocation, a beckoning magic for Cora's and Anthony's children.

My grandchildren.

But I would never get the chance to know them.

They would only ever hear of me in the past tense.

I gave a small smile to myself.

Jimmy would never think of himself as among the heroes.

He belongs in such elite company. He will for ever remain a true icon in my mind in this world and the next.

My small smile turned into a small tear.

Jimmy would have to be the curator of my memories.

A vein of grief runs through my life now. I have made the discovery that grief could attach itself with permanence. It attached itself and then it burrowed inside and made a nest and lingered like an unwelcome guest. It ate whatever was warm in the chambers of the heart, and then the coldness settled in permanently. This is the wound that never really heals, but each in their own unique way learns to live with it, with greater or lesser success.

Death ends a life but not a relationship. Memory becomes your partner. You nurture it. You hold it. You dance with it.

My absence would become a presence for my soon-to-be widowed husband. Memory is our way of holding on to those we love. Jimmy has left me a treasure trove of memories. Without him, my world is a poorer and duller place.

It was one of the great blessings of my life to have him as my husband. My greatest blessing, though, was to have been his friend for over twenty years.

The life of the dead is placed in the memories of the living. The love we feel in life keeps people alive beyond their time. Anyone who has given love will always live on in another's heart. The stars in the sky are not the eyes of God but the stars of those who have passed on, lovingly watching over us.

I hoped my star would shine the brightest for Jimmy.

I whispered six words.

Goodbye to you, my trusted friend.

*That Evening: Back Home in Athlone*

All has changed.

All has changed utterly.

Or am I dreaming?

Could a miracle really have happened to me?

# 2

# Rock Bottom

*'. . . for Christ plays in ten thousand places,*
*Lovely in limbs, and lovely in eyes not his . . .'*

— GERARD MANLEY HOPKINS, 'As Kingfishers Catch Fire'

Please Lord, don't let me die just yet. All I ask you is to let me live long enough to see my children grow into maturity.

It was a cry of the heart — a prayer born not out of selfishness but out of love and faith. On the third of September 1989 I was in my wheelchair as part of a diocesan pilgrimage to Knock. As I looked up at the statute of Our Blessed Lady at Knock, I seemed to the outside world to be just another pilgrim. In that setting, my story was not unusual. I was on a stretcher, suffering from a crippling illness, small in stature, of gentle disposition, someone who obviously had been afflicted by a heavy cross in life. Like so many others, I was seen by family and friends as a special gift of God to those who came into contact with me.

Yet, as my illness was becoming increasingly more debilitating, it seemed to those who knew me that the time was fast approaching when I had to be offered back to God; for it was with God that I surely belonged and it was only in God that I would find the peace I longed for in life.

As I looked around me in the packed basilica, I saw the many faces of human suffering. In some of my darker moments I had asked the question in prayer: 'Why Me, Lord?' At least in Knock I felt I was not suffering on my own. Some were suffering physically and, like myself, were on stretchers. I wondered if some of the emaciated bodies were victims of cancer.

The heavily lined faces and sad eyes of others suggested great mental and emotional pressure to me. Was it depression, marital breakdown, child–parent conflicts, shattered dreams, crippling financial problems, long-term unemployment, poverty, overcrowding or lack of educational opportunity that produced so many heavy hearts? A sentence from Mother Teresa flashed through my mind in which she described loneliness as the biggest cause of suffering in our time. Despite my discomfort I felt lucky, graced by a loving God. I had been blessed by so much love.


## For it Is When I Am Weak that I Am Strong

Again, I thought of death and how it would affect my young children. I knew that, although I was able to actually do very little for my family, they would suffer greatly from my absence. I appreciated that my life was by no means useless or of little value. On the contrary, it had a value beyond compare, a value which I could not measure, which only time and eternity would reveal fully. For my children, my value was not what their mother could or could not do but, more importantly, in what and who she was. They saw me as a child of God and, in my simplicity and vulnerability, they discovered that people come first and that much happiness can be found in making time for each other. I brought out the best of each of them, I hoped, binding them together and bringing them joy.

*Happier Times*

I smiled to myself as I remembered the day I got married to Jimmy.
I had been so blissfully happy. The world seemed our oyster. Our
new lives together had promised nothing but chapters of happiness.
Yet the dream had turned into a nightmare; illness had sucked away
my energy and vitality.

Yet neither the foundation nor rich architecture of my faith had
been threatened. The very opposite was the case.

The basilica was full of holy people – so called 'ordinary people'
whose generosity towards God was as tangible a sign of divine love
as anyone was ever entitled to expect. Down through the history of
the Christian faith, many people have been considered good, such
as Jesus Christ, St Francis of Assisi and Mother Teresa. What is
noteworthy about these people, their great moments apart, is that it
is their simplicity which chiefly colours our conception of them. On
closer examination, we see that their lives were full of frailty. Their
value could not be measured by a spiritual balance sheet – doing
more and doing it better – but by being a worthy ambassador for
God's people, by leading lives which had a definite direction about
them, a goal and a unity of purpose. Frailty and holiness went hand
in hand on that Sunday in Knock.

I felt I was on holy ground – each stone, each blade of grass
outside, each singing bird flying over the basilica, each voice, each
smiling face, each concerned look, all and each, each and all, were
holy, radiant ornaments on the sacred altar of creation, jewels in
God's sanctuary. I felt comfort in the thought that, although all is
passing, all is eternal. In the stillness of my soul I sensed the eternal
movement, in the tireless movement of the energetic children with
their thoughts on sugar sticks and chocolate, I saw deeper into the
abundant calm. In that moment the harsh overtures of my rampaging

illness were dissolved and I was a child again. It was a magic moment. All the world was in tune with my heart.

## The Pietà

All of us who have lost a loved one know what it is like to experience a hidden grieving that rises to grab the heart. We are occasionally ambushed by painful emotions.

Many of us know what it is like to be pelted with sorrow. Inevitably, in times of suffering, we experience moments of doubt. This is not unusual. Jesus himself suffered from uncertainty. At the wedding feast of Cana, Jesus initially did not want to perform the miracle of turning water into wine because he did not believe he could. He was only spurred into action when Mary said to him, 'Do you not know yet who you are?'

On that day in Knock I found myself thinking of Mary the Mother of God. However, it was not the holy woman whose picture we see on countless Christmas cards. Instead it was the Mary of Michelangelo's statue of a woman and her son. This is *The Pietà*, depicting the Mother of Jesus, holding the body of her dead son in her arms. In *The Pietà*, we see great love and strength, but equally a heart-wrenching moment of lamentation and agony at life's capacity for cruelty. This Mary speaks loudly of suffering, of pain, of agony.

While Mary recognised God's love and had hope in the power of God working in her life, she had to live with the imperfections of the present. She is united today with all people who suffer – by an openness to allowing God to grow in their lives and in their sadness. God grows in them as in Mary – though, like a seed in winter, He grows silently, most often in darkness, so that frequently they could not recognise what was happening. Often it was only in retrospect that they could see signs of the divine presence.

While Mary was honoured with the greatest gift of all, she also had her own trials and tribulations. She received the Good News at the Annunciation, but she also had to watch her son suffer in agony on the cross at Calvary. Her gifts were matched by her crosses. In this way she is close to our own lives – which are their own unique mixtures of joy and sadness.

Mary wondered and reflected as she nurtured the child growing within her. We often think of Mary as different from ourselves. But, reflecting on her life, we discover that she herself walked in darkness and uncertainty before us. She herself has known our fears and insecurities. That is why we can turn to her with confidence in our moments of crisis.

This does not mean that all our problems will melt away. Rather Mary points us to a new reality which will give us the strength to face up to the harsh aspects of modern life, to experience and to transmit the touch of God's gentle love. The message of Mary is not that we get a ladder to climb up to heaven – but instead we have joy because God has come down from heaven to raise us up to new heights.

I like to remember Mary. She understands our suffering but is also a woman of hope. She invites us to place our trust in God, who never leaves us or abandons us. She was open to learning from all her experiences and came to understand that God speaks to us through all the events of our lives, be they good or bad. In this way we can face the future with confidence, knowing that God will give us what we need for each day. It is through the gift of life that we can understand the meaning of love and relationships between all people; through our own suffering we are comforted and through our comfort we learn to love everybody.

## *Shadows and Light*

It was exhilarating to feel this inner peace that my heart had hungered for, a hunger that could only be satisfied with a loving God. I cherished the thought, but such a union could not be found in this world. A tidal wave of happiness swept over me as I thought of God in heaven. But my joy was short-lived. I saw my family before me again. I thought of my bonds of love with them, my gratitude at all they had done for me and given me, my constant wonder at the mystery of their unending goodness and their need for me. My mood underwent a sea-change: hanging desperately on to life for the sake of my children became everything for me. I had often heard people saying 'hope springs eternal' but, at that precise second, hope seemed a nonsense.

It was difficult not to feel sad. As I sat listlessly on the stretcher, more memories of my life with Jimmy came flooding back to me. Sweet memories were recalled with affection. All the 'might-have-beens' were discarded wistfully. The moments of tragedy and heart-break were quickly brushed to one side. I wanted to live with an intensity that was almost frightening. Like seeds dreaming of spring beneath the snow, my heart dreamed that I would get a few more years, but medical advice suggested that this was futile. The shadow of death lurked ominously over me like a vulture hovering over its prey. I forced myself to think positively. The sound of pilgrims praying was soothing, almost hypnotic.

Reading back over my diary about those dark moments, it is not what I said that is so revealing. What strikes me most forcefully is not the words or even the story itself, but the raw emotion. Words cannot do justice to the depth of my feeling. There were protracted pauses. Uncharacteristically, the words come slowly, almost tortu-ously. It is as if I am re-living every second of those moments which remain firmly entrenched in my brain.

Because of my illness I could never hold my second baby in my arms. None of the physical pain or mental distress I endured compared with the nightmare of being a mother incapable of 'real' mothering.

It would be easy to talk about my condition as a modern-day tragedy. Much too easy. Greatness is most obviously manifest in the face of adversity. There would have been no benefit to my children if I fell victim to the 'why me?' syndrome or the futility of the 'what-might-have-been' mentality and thus become paralysed with self-pity. Not me. I have overcome my personal misfortune and rather than brood on the past my concern is to make up for lost time. Each new day is an opportunity to redress the balance and restore the correct relationship between a mother and her children.

## The Road to Calvary and Back

I now see this time of intense suffering as a source of blessing. Adversity brought even greater unity among my family. It opened our eyes to the wonder of ordinary life and the beauty of the Athlone countryside around us. The newly born lambs which speckled the fields in the springtime as they chased each other playfully were savoured anew. The daffodils which enveloped the lawns like yellow blankets elicited smiles of pleasure again.

It is like seeing everything with new eyes. My suffering was difficult, unpleasant, painful, but, as Jesus proved on Good Friday, it can be much more. It also presented me with a wonderful opportunity: a chance to embrace the Jesus of Good Friday, who suffered Himself, and is furiously tender to the damaged and the weak.

Only a God who had been crucified, though totally innocent of all that he was accused of, and who truly suffered death as a man, could have understood what I was going through on that Sunday in Knock. As I looked up at the image of His battered body on the crucifix in the basilica, I saw the parallels between my own life and Good Friday. Like Jesus himself I had been humiliated, rejected by people who had once called me 'friend', stripped of everything which gives life meaning.

I had carried my own cross, had my own Good Friday experience, but I did not feel ready for my Easter Sunday. I had walked with Jesus to Calvary and beyond. In my frail, emaciated body, God's grace had shone like a diamond. For all the pain and darkness of my previous seventeen years on earth, I knew deep down that I was a child of God's light and delight. When the time was right, I too would have the glory of the resurrection when I would rise with the Son. The sorrowful mysteries would become joyful and glorious.

Not for the first time I experienced within myself the internal struggle of the human heart to purify itself of selfishness and small-ness and open itself to love. Was it really selfish to want to live a little longer for the sake of my children? Or was I flying in the face of the will of God in asking to live a little longer? I prayed that my heart would always be as large and spacious as the crashing Atlantic Ocean just a few miles away. It never occurred to me to pray for a cure.

For seventeen years I had been in the chains of physical illness, struck down by Multiple Sclerosis and a proliferation of ailments. My kidneys no longer functioned, I was blind in one eye, paralysed down one side, had epilepsy, slurred speech and thyroid trouble. I had to eat my food either liquidised or cut into small pieces. It was as if my entire body was giving up, abandoning a drowning ship.

But life is full of promise. Even in the depths of winter the promise of spring brings new hope, dawn follows the darkest night; war will give way to peace and even from the most negative experience seeds of possibility sprout forth. As I looked into the jaws of death, a miracle lay just around the corner and a level of joy and exhilaration I had never even dreamed of carried me away on a tide of magical memories.

I glow contentedly as I remember the day that changed my life.


*Bound in Love*

As always at Knock, the Mass was a moving occasion, a Holy Communion of saints and sinners. No additional words were necessary. The devout faces told their own story.

The service was dignified and proper, but it was the consecration which will live for ever in my memory. It had always been the crucial part of the Mass for me in which I always strove to give my undivided attention believing that there can be no consecration without concentration. It was a very poignant moment. The atmosphere was reverential.

The chief celebrant was my bishop, Bishop Colm O'Reilly. It was a Mass like any other special Mass in Knock, or so it seemed. One of life's most irritating yet exciting qualities is its unpredictability. For long periods it can run smoothly and follow the projected direction, but then events arise out of the blue which involve a radical readjustment. The next few moments would transform life for me and my entire family.

After receiving the body of Christ, it slowly dawned on me that all the pain had left my body. I could not be cured, could I? I came as a 'cripple'; it was too much to expect that I could walk. I knew it was foolish, but after a long struggle to overcome my fear of looking foolish, I asked after Mass that the stretcher be opened.

The stretcher was opened with uncertainty and with extraordinary tenderness.

I stood up.

A miracle had happened.

I could walk.

It was as if I was born again.

# 3

# A Foreign Country

*'Love seeketh not Itself to please,*
*Nor for itself hath any care;*
*But for another gives its ease,*
*And builds a Heaven in Hell's despair.'*

— WILLIAM BLAKE, 'The Clod and the Pebble'

Who was it who said that the past is a foreign country?

We are all a product of our times. I grew up in a very different Ireland. It was a time when, like the famous D'Unbelievables sketch, you had to go to Mass early if you did not want to take a seat.

I was the first child of Joe and Pauline McCormack. Mine is the story of a bygone age when life moved at a gentler pace and there always seemed to be time for chat and laughter.

This was life for an extremely hard-working, relatively prosperous, family, in a provincial town. Nestling on the banks of the Shannon, Athlone was the gateway to the historical province of Connacht, or the road to Dublin, depending on your starting point. It was an age of innocence, as typified in the giving of directions to wayward motorists:

'Could you tell me the road to Mullingar please?'

'Well indeed I can. But let me tell you if I were you, I wouldn't start from here at all.'

The Shannon river itself provided a source of enduring fascination to the young Marion McCormack, with its seasonal music, as it ebbed and flowed when the weather was calm, or as it hurled itself under the impressive bridge on stormy days. Ireland's longest river poured forth contradictory symphonies of unrestrained welcome and spine-chilling fear.

Athlone was a town of narrow streets, which, in later years, would be the cause of interminable traffic jams, particularly on wet Friday evenings. At the centre was a bridge which straddled two parts of town life – the market town which brought farmers in from neighbouring hinterlands like Curraghboy, Kiltoom, Rahara and Dysart and the industrial centre which was spawning a series of new factories as Ireland slowly and tortuously caught up with the industrial revolution like a marathon runner finally on his last lap.

For the vast majority of people in the town there were three pillars in life: family, work and God. Even in towns like Athlone the sense of community was very strong, if not quite as rocklike as in the surrounding country areas. For example, many families still made their own butter. It was always the job of 'the woman of the house', her mottled hands gripping the long handle going through the lid of the barrel-shaped churn as she pumped the milk into butter. It was energy-sapping work as the pale clots of butter floated on the steaming milk or stuck to the grain in the sides of the wooden churn. Of course, people also made their own bread, and I can still see the cross on my mother's cakes. The odd time, a few currants were thrown in and we ended up with currant cake which was a real treat.

People seldom socialised formally – in those days only the gentry did that sort of thing. In the main, people's outings were when they went to Mass on Sundays. The kettle was always on the boil for the obligatory greeting when friend, causal caller or total stranger called: 'Sit down there by the fire. Ah sure you'll have a cup of tea in your hand.' People never seemed to be put out when the stranger called unexpectedly, inevitably at the most awkward times.

## Leaving Erin's Shore

Athlone, and its surrounding area, suffered the curse of emigration in the 1950s because the holdings were uneconomic. The saddest part of life was to watch families, or parts of families, going away to London for the building sites or to Scotland for the potato picking. Many who spent just a few years in London returned with an accent that was more Cockney than 'Athlonesque'. The local wits observed, 'He is only gone a wet week and already he is back with a fancy accent.'

The shadow of emigration lurked like a dark cloud over all of us. It was central to the culture of the west of Ireland – and not unfamiliar to us; the traditional Irish solution to economic problems. It churned out an assembly line of bodies for the boat to England and America.

Emigration stripped communities of their young people in the same way a flock of sheep would demolish a field of fresh grass. It shaped the way people thought and felt, conditioning them to accept the grotesquely abnormal as normal. That was the way it was, and that was the way it would always be. Although there were no industries, there was one highly developed export: people.

There were many scenes of families travelling en masse to the train station. Everyone wore their Sunday best. The mother was blind with tears. The father's eyes were dry, but his heart was breaking. For of course, men did not betray emotion. It would have been seen as a sign of weakness. The young people leaving leaned out of the windows, choking with sadness as they saw their parents for perhaps the last time. Younger brothers and sisters raced after the train shouting words of parting. Sometimes white handkerchiefs were produced and waved until the train went out of sight. Those handkerchiefs gave a ritual, almost sacramental, solemnity, to the goodbyes. Their presence was a symbol of defeat, a damning indictment of an economy unable to provide for its brightest and most talented.

Hundreds of young and not-so-young people left every year. The collective tale of woe concealed thousands of individual nightmares. Young people wanted to stay in the country they loved, but they had no way of making a living. They wanted to be close to family and friends, but they had no other choice but to leave. Many had good skills. Some had excellent examination results. Yet the piece of paper that was most important was the ticket to America.

## Early Days

Snow fell the day of my birth. It was a difficult labour.

Were it not for the midwifery skills of a family friend, Peggy Egan, I would not be alive. I was born and reared in the Old Batteries in Athlone. My early memories are of my grannie and of a holy picture of Our Lady of Lourdes. I also vividly recall when my grand-uncle Jack called to our house and showed me the centre page of *Woman's Own* on which there was a picture of a young girl with curly hair. He told me it was a photo of me. I was full sure it was me and it was years later before I discovered he was pulling my leg.

I was an only child for eight years, but then three brothers, Jimmy, Shane and David and a sister, Jacinta, were born. There are eighteen years between Jacinta and me. When I was very young, my mother and father went to work in England for a year or two. My grandparents looked after me. My grandfather worked in Lysters' sawmill. I loved going for walks with him. He built me a beautiful doll's house. My grandmother was a great cook who baked lovely bread. I can still see her making toast in front of the range. She had long hair with massive curls.

My best friend was Lily Berrigan – who tragically died in 1983 at a young age. We loved the same things, even the same songs, like Cliff Richard's 'Congratulations'. We promised that if she had a son and I had a daughter or vice versa then they would be married and we would be related. Every Saturday night we went together to Kilroy's sweetshop in Connacht Street for an ice pop. I remember, too, buying Brylcreem for my uncle Peter. Sunday afternoon was for attending the Ritz cinema with four old pence for the entry fee to the matinee. Although I was not afraid of death, I developed an awful fear of being buried alive from watching too many Dracula films.

The Old Batteries, a stretch of land just outside the town, were the greatest adventure ground anywhere. In winter, during the time of a big snow, we sped down the hill on the bonnet of a Morris Minor. I also remember taking the lid of my mother's washing machine and sliding down the hill – of course, totally forgetting the fact that I was sure to scrape the lid in the process. My mother, as you would expect, was less than pleased – and that's putting it mildly. Another day I remember climbing to the top of the scaffolding on the water tower.

I had many moments of loneliness in my childhood, but Jesus and Mary were always there for me. My aunt Margaret bought me a beautiful prayer book and whenever I felt down, I turned to Mary. I once got a present of a book on etiquette and had great fun finding out what was the 'right thing'. My grandmother gave me a great love of the books of Walter Macken. I remember learning that when the seagulls came inland it was a sign of bad weather and that someone once said that the stars are the poetry of heaven.

My father served in the British army during the Second World War and it was from him that I got my love of music. But both my parents were big music fans and talked a lot about the American singer, Mario Lanza. Michael Collins was the other name often discussed in our home.

Growing up, I was very conscious of the fact that I was from a very privileged family. I always knew that I had more money than most of my friends, but I was never conscious of the fact that other people lived in poverty. I had nice clothes and a bike and can never remember any of us wanting anything. My parents worked very hard and put in long hours. That was the time when it was considered that you were a good parent if you were a good provider. My mother didn't get home until half six in the evening. As a young girl I can remember never dreaming of anything other than having my mother home to meet me when I came home from school. It was a really special day if she had a half-day and met me as I came home. Normally it was the other way around.

## Hallowed Be Thy Name

I suppose in the Ireland I grew up in, religion was a very strong influence. We had a Sacred Heart lamp in our kitchen and we changed the flowers regularly. I'm not sure what it instilled in us, but it was part of our background.

Every day, my mother rounded us all up to say the Rosary, and I can remember arguments going on and kicks under the chair as the

Rosary was said. I can remember looking out the window as a way of getting through the Rosary, so I'm not sure there was much piety involved there!

My mother was a very traditional Catholic. Others had a totally different approach. This God could be found out in the fields and was seen as part of nature. I always appreciated the God of the fields and the God of nature. It was just part of us. A few people would sit down when they had breakfast on Sunday morning and they would turn on the radio and listen to religious services on the BBC, which was kind of unusual, and would always say, 'Listen to what's going on now because you'll be hearing the exact same in our own church.' They would always feel that no one and no group had a right to take hold of God.

Like so many, I found it easy to find God in nature. One thing that really takes hold of my mind is the rogation days. I think it was the three minor days before the Ascension. Farmers would go out in the evenings and bless the crops. I love the sense that there was nobody there between them and their own land and God; as they asked God to bless their work. It was a lovely custom and brought God very close to them in the fields. People also went out into their own gardens and blessed them with Holy Water on the major Rogation Day. I realised then that, when you grow up, you do absorb this understanding, even though you may not be conscious of it at the time. It colours your life afterwards.

Sunday was always a leisurely day for us in the McCormack household. There was always time for a good long chat after Mass. I retain vivid memories of Sunday mornings in Athlone when gleaming lines of family cars graced the car park below the church. The church bell tolled, calling the respectable, responsible citizens of the townland to worship. The late-comers frantically scampered up the steps, slipping red-faced into a seat at the back, momentarily disturbing the hushed stillness. Men in dark overcoats shuffled in the porch whispering about the price of cattle over the prayers. Local gossip was traded. Women in their best coats with righteous heads held high thought of the Sunday dinner. Having endured the compulsory fast before Communion, many tummies were rumbling. Outside, the children's screams pierced the frosty air.

## Shoe the Donkey

Toys, for most kids, were very scarce and the children depended on their imagination for amusement. They played hoops with old cart-wheels. Another pastime was making primitive spinning tops. These were simply small cone-shaped, brightly coloured pieces of wood. A second piece of wood with a narrow leather strap was used as the top to get it to spin. The winner was the one whose top would spin the longest. The boys played toss-the-penny, on the rare occasions when there was a penny available. Usually small stones provided an acceptable substitute. Another game was skimming stones on a pond. The daredevils' greatest mischief was robbing apples in the autumn. The girls learned some of the great Irish dances like 'Shoe the Donkey'.

Children were real tearaways, with the abrasiveness that comes when natural ebullience chafes against acquired cynicism, stampeding through the Batteries like bolshie ponies – interested only in happiness. They rushed into life headlong, all frenzied energy and defiance. However, it was above all a world of respect. If youngsters were on the rope, like prize fighters they were pinged back to the centre of the ring by their parents with deceptive ease and watchful delicacy, miracles of watchful warmth and worldly innocence. When children got out of control they were threatened with the 'pookey man'.

Our family did a lot of entertaining. It was a pre-television era, the era of rambling. When the evening meal was over, the day's work done, the Family Rosary finished, people gathered to chat and tell stories. When the visitors arrived, the chairs were moved back, and the circle increased. News was spread and the news tended to give the lead for the night's subject, money, death, health or sickness. All was grist to the mill – the praise for the dead and the doings of the living.

The best storytellers were artists, who could at once switch from gravity to gaiety. They were light-hearted people, and their changes of mood and face were like the changes of running water, with a penchant for performing, enlivening dour narratives with adventurous digressions. They were loquacious, self-deprecating and possessed a medium-to-dry sense of humour. As they talked, their hands would be working too; a little clap of the palms to cap a phrase, a flash of the thumb over their shoulders to mark a mystery, a hand hushed to mouth for mischief or whispered secrecy. Yarn followed yarn, and while one was telling one story, the other was thinking up a 'good one' to follow. The anecdotes were very good, clean and innocent and, in most of them, there was a grain of truth, so it was difficult not to believe them. Ghost stories were incredibly popular and would scare the pants off you. I was less keen, though, on the proliferation of stories about the brutality of the Black and Tans.

According to the old Irish proverb, 'When the fun is at its height, it's time to go.'

And, at such a time, the ritual in most of the rambling houses was to draw the ashes over the peat embers to preserve the fire with a customary prayer:

'I preserve the fire as Christ preserves all. Brigid at the two ends of the house, and Mary in the centre. The three angels and the three apostles who are highest in the Kingdom of Grace, guarding this house and its contents until day.'

Neighbours also visited one another's houses to hold card-playing sessions. Ten men might play 'twenty-five' – five sets of partners. Sometimes a row would start after a round because some man's partner had not played the deuce of diamonds or the five of spades. This card playing was treated as a matter of life and death. Some men had reputations as fine card players, and this was something to be guarded jealously.

For adults the possibilities for alternative entertainment were expanding. Dances brought husband and wife together in a playful atmosphere which fanned the flickering flames of romance. Always pragmatists, the local canons or parish priests saw the mercenary advantages of having a weekly dance. Like the poor, the parish debt was and is always with us. Grandiose projects for the church required finance. Never one to miss an opportunity, the priests frequently decided to establish weekly bingo sessions. In pursuit of the general good, they put aside their private reservations that bingo was so intellectually lightweight as to be psychologically dangerous and plain silly. They persuaded themselves that bingo was a blessing for those who, because of circumstances outside their control, were destined to live enormously uneventful lives.

New influences were seeping into the lives of the locals in the guise of modernity.

As everyone proudly said in those parts, 'Home is home.' This cryptic saying means that home is far better than all those places you could see on the television and that the blanket of green in which it wallows, sometimes uncomfortably, is to be preferred to the paved streets of the best cities of the world. Can anybody disagree with logic like that? To dissent is to be disloyal to communal wisdom and to be disloyal to that wisdom, so carefully and painstakingly distilled through the ages, is arrogance. And arrogance is the eighth deadly sin.

## Through the Fields

We lived in the town, but country life was all around us. The 1960s were a time when the whitewashed houses with thatched roofs peeped furtively out of the butter-brown bog. It was a beautiful country, with a majestic and powerful sweep to it, but it yielded precious little to some of those who lived at the heart of it. There was plenty of rain, plenty of bog, but an acute shortage of people, especially young people. As was the case throughout rural Ireland, land had cultural and spiritual connotations in addition to economic significance. The Catholic faith, like the land, was passed on from one generation to the next. Both land and faith lay at the heart of the community.

The harsh terrain and small farms made survival difficult. People had very little to celebrate. The only escape, at least for the men, from the problems and anxieties of everyday living lay in football. It allowed them to dream of better days to come. Success at either parish or county level, albeit on a very modest scale, increased people's self-esteem. They talked just a little more boldly, they walked that little bit taller, and they waved their flags with pride. It is impossible to explain the intense, almost tribal loyalty which genuine followers of GAA give to the team. There was close identification between the fans and the players. The players represented the community. The GAA was part of what and who the community was. As Fr Harry Bohan said, 'That was all we had. Mass and the match.'

## The Voice

The All-Ireland final is one of the last genuine folk festivals left to us. There is no lens wide enough or screen big enough to take in its uniqueness, the ritual and razzmatazz and throbbing public excitement of it all. Who could resist its rustic charm? In all sport, there is no arena to match it. It is a place where the pressures of normal life are suspended, a theatre of dreams, stirring abiding memories in its devotees who recall unforgettable moments and evoke memories of the greats and of less well-known players against which the great drama of sport is played out. It has unlimited potential for excitement, drama, tension, spectacle, elation and bitter disappointment, all packaged together – though never neatly. History never stops, but the All-Ireland final hits the pause button for moments of basking in the glories of yesteryear. Tradition is an essential ingredient in hurling's sporting dish.

Like so many of my generation I was converted to Gaelic games by the GAA's answer to St Paul, Micheál O'Hehir. His conversions did not take place on the road to Damascus but from the 'magic box' on kitchen tables throughout the country. People of my generation remember the enormity of the occasion when they got their first radio, the magic of listening to programmes like *The Foley Family*, *The Kennedys of Castleross*, *Hospitals Requests* and stories told by the *seanachaí*, Eamon Kelly.

Micheál O'Hehir was the man who brought Gaelic games in vivid form to the people of Ireland at a time when television was unknown and transistors unheard of. Growing up, there were few distractions apart from the wireless, with the wet batteries and dry batteries, and of course we listened to O'Hehir's commentaries religiously. Listening to the radio, we never saw those great players, but Micheál, who really made the GAA, turned them into superheroes.

He showed that hurling and football and games are an art apart; their extent and depth perhaps not fully realised, rather merely accepted. He was a national institution. His voice could stay calm, mellifluous and charged with relevant information in the most thrilling contest – the perfect instrument for putting names and personalities to the blurred rainbow of a heart-stopping match. He was as much part of the furniture of the lives of Gaelic games' fans as religion and politics.

As we marched, not always successfully, to the relentless demands of a faster, more superficial age, just to hear his voice was to know that all was well with the world. He painted pictures with words like a master craftsman. Young boys listening to him decided immediately that they wanted to join the ranks of the football and hurling immortals. Nobody ever did more for the GAA than him. Seldom has one man brought so much joy and inspiration to so many. If enthusiasm was electricity, Micheál would have been a power station. He was quite simply *the* voice.

And after Dana won the Eurovision in 1970, we all became more interested in music. Radio was part of the furniture of people's lives. Everybody had their own favourites, but one programme was compulsive listening in our house when we were children, and that was Santa's journey from the North Pole on Christmas Eve.

## Power to *All Our Friends*

Even in the late 1960s and early 1970s, the legacy of the civil war still lingered in Athlone. Heated exchanges between neighbours on the merits and demerits of the polices of the two parties *Fianna Fáil* and *Fine Gael* were a regular occurrence. On election day, party activists spent the entire day in the local polling station as observers, ensuring that nobody from the other side would try something underhand like voting twice. There was also a more positive purpose: to ensure that all the party faithful 'did the right thing'. Everybody in the parish knew how about four-fifths of the parish voted. A good indication was provided at Mass on Sunday when people bought the Sunday papers: the Fine Gaelers bought *The Sunday Independent*, while the Fianna Fáilers took *The Sunday Press*.

Equality of the sexes was not yet a feature of Irish elections. Although women's rights were being recognised by a series of legislative measures, party activists concentrated their energies on the male voters, based on the theory that the men would always keep the women in line. This was a very simplistic proposition. Another presumption, which sometimes led to inaccurate conclusions, was assuming that a particular voter's decision to travel in a particular party's car indicated support for that party.

Once the voter walked into the polling station, they were watched like hawks. A discreet nod was passed between the voter and the 'party man', to signify that the duty would be discharged in the expected fashion. A tell-tale sign was when a traditional party supporter was unable to make eye contact with their observer. This meant they had transferred their allegiance to the other side. News of this turncoat's treachery was quickly communicated to party bosses in the area. Within hours, the whole parish knew about it. When I learned in school about the secret ballot, I thought the people who came up with the idea would have to devise something far more sophisticated for rural Ireland.

It always amuses me when I hear people saying that, unlike the British, we don't have a class system. That's not true; we have something much more subtle. In rural Ireland there was a very definite hierarchy, which kept everybody in their preordained

niche. The only way to break free from your appointed status was
to move out.

## A Day Out

Most families went to the Carn Park bog, just outside of Athlone.
Although the bog can be backbreaking work, there is something
special, almost spiritual about it. The scent of turf fires and bog tea
was a sensory pleasure. All human life was there. Women, men,
young, old, happy, sad, the industrious and the lethargic. Although
it was a very exposed terrain if the weather was nasty, when the
sun was shining, I always felt that God was smiling on the world.
Everything was in harmony. It was my very own garden of Eden.

Although breakfast after first Mass on Sunday morning was
conducted in semi-silence in deference to Ciarán Mac Mathúna
on the wireless, my father's favourite music was birds singing. He
especially loved the cuckoo, which sent its voice of mystery from out
the woodland depths and wide-open spaces calling nature to rejoice
at the advent of spring.

The song of the cuckoo was an echo of the halcyon days in paradise, rendering nature what it truly is – beautiful, poetic life at its
innocent best, the world as it ought to be, the ideal for a moment
realised. As we took refuge in a canopy of trees during April showers
everything seemed made from memory. The sound of the cuckoo
enshrouded us with a redemptive feeling, melting away depression,
pain and bitter disappointment. The cuckoo's dulcet tones hinted at
a bygone age of innocence and values that no longer obtain. The
music was sweet and sensual, evocative of a higher world.

Then, with EEC membership in 1973, the point of demarcation
between farming and commerce became harder to identify. These

changes were not all to our advantage. One of the unforeseen conse-
quences was that the sounds of our outside world changed. I always
loved, on a warm June evening, listening to the warm milk squirting
into the pail when I saw one of our friends milking the cows. Most of
the animals were docile creatures. They allowed farmers to crouch
on the stool and, with heads against their flanks, to effortlessly send a
white milky jet hissing and frothing into the bucket. Soon that music
was replaced by the dull droning of the plague of clinical, time-
efficient milking machines that infested the area.

When Ireland joined the EEC, *The Farmer's Journal* became not
just an optional extra but a constituent part of agricultural life in
rural Ireland in a fundamentally formative sense. Ireland had moved
into the big league and, if farmers were to prosper, they needed
to recognise that the old ways which had served well in the 1950s
would no longer be adequate to a fast-changing reality. *The Farmer's
Journal* was the window which reflected the new opportunities and
challenges, and the benefits of adopting innovatory methods. Above
all, it consistently hammered home the message that the recipe for
success in farming lay in good management.

EEC membership brought a new vocabulary of its own 'headage
payments', 'subsistence grants', 'maintenance grants' and 'Brussels
bureaucrats'. Farmers loved the EEC because it meant lovely grants,
grants for reclaiming marshy land and grants for new farm buildings. Someone once said, 'The EEC would give you a grant for
sneezing loudly.' It was as if all farmers' Christmases had come at
once. A visible air of prosperity was evident around the country.
The new cars got bigger. Some people went on holidays and one or
two colour televisions were purchased.

From my father's point of view, the most disappointing feature
of the change of landscape was the virtual disappearance of the

corncrake. These secretive little birds were the victims of progress: when silage came in, their natural habitat was destroyed. It was my father who first introduced me to the sweet sound of the corncrake. Once we had gone out in the still night to check for the stars, we drank together from the bird's symphony of raucous notes pleading in the night. The corncrake seemed to bring not just good tidings but elation. I always associated that sound with sun-drenched summers in the age of my innocence and youth.

Memory is blurred and softened by time, but I always remember those summers as times of perpetual sunshine, bright moonscapes and the sound of laughter. I wondered if the corncrake suffered from insomnia; he always seemed to be in full voice just as everyone else was trying to sleep. Even so, I often cursed the age of silage for depriving me not just of the corncrake but of all the nostalgia, wide-eyed simplicity and the unadulterated happiness and excitement of childhood.

The countryside smells changed, too. I was never crazy about the scent of horse dung, but it was infinitely preferable to the pollution and impregnating smoke of tractors and heavy agricultural machinery. The sweet smell of hay was a sensory, almost sinfully sensual pleasure. By comparison the assault on one's nose by silage was vulgar. In the haymaking season it always seemed that all the scents of the earth and growing things which had been imprisoned were released by the summer sunshine in waves of piercing sweetness.

Tastes were changing, too. Around this time farming children almost provoked a riot when they announced to their parents' horror that they would no longer drink 'cow's milk' or eat homemade butter. When questioned as to where the milk would come from, they replied in all sincerity, 'From a bottle in the shop.'

My favourite season was spring when the trees hummed with

contentment. Rabbits made love in fields that proudly displayed their blankets of green. Thoughts of liberation filled all minds. Miracles of rebirth.

Summer was the season for mushrooms. I woke up early in the mornings during August to go out mushroom-picking under the warm glow of the rising sun before gathering cows for the milking. I learned quickly that most valuable skill for any practitioner of my new profession – how to tell a field which would yield mushrooms from one which would not. Now and then I would reach treasure island – a seemingly limitless, just-popped bunch of pure white mushrooms lovingly caressing the green grass.

## Caring and Sharing

One of our neighbours killed pigs at the weekend for the princely sum of a pound: doing the first half of the job on Saturday afternoon, actually killing the pig, and finishing it on the Sunday and curing the bacon. Some of the bacon was hung up the chimney and was smoked in the process. Half the homes cured bacon; the pork steaks and the pudding went around the countryside. Everyone got some of it and by the time it was distributed there was little left for the pig's owner but still no one went hungry and that was what real Christianity was about, giving and sharing.

My father was very partial to blackberries. I quickly acquired this taste, but reaching for the most luscious blackberries was a hazardous experience when they were shielded by an almost impenetrable fortress of briars. The price for my snacks were a few scratches on my hand and quite a few tears on my clothing, a tendency which did not endear me to my mother. Another culinary delight was digging the early potatoes in June, just watching the white skins coming out of the clay was enough to make me lick my lips. Little things were big adventures like collecting one-day-old chicks off the bus and bringing them home.

Autumn was the harvest – when we picked potatoes using old socks for gloves on damp, chilly evenings. Another autumnal story was when the thresher came to each family farm. It is difficult to believe that just fifty years ago the thresher was a central part of life in rural Ireland, but now it is just a museum piece, since replaced by combine harvesters.

Fair Days were big events in Athlone and in all rural towns like Ballygar, where there was a fair on the eighteenth of every month. The town was a hive of activity, with dogs barking, farmers roaring, cattle lowing, sheep straying into the wrong places. Chaos ensued when one farmer's flock became intermingled with another's. Inevitably a major row resulted as both parties attempted to place blame for the misadventure onto the other.

The farmers in attendance were artists in their own line – their line being cattle and sheep. Animals were bought and sold at the fairs, not just for money but because these farmers enjoyed the handling of them, the business of attending sales and the slow, shrewd talk of men as knowledgeable as themselves. They talked as if talk were what had been denied to them all, as if they were starving for it.

Old controversies emerged from their caves of obscurity and were delicately excavated. Many of the men went home the scenic route – via the pub.

They were, in the main, tough, shrewd farmers who seemed ageless, for sun and hard work and good eating had shaped their bodies into cases of muscle that time could hardly touch. This was their life for years: one of exhausting physical toil, twelve hours a day of sweat and effort in the sun. On a fair day an ill-chosen phrase could see a farmer emitting the sort of body language that would have made the most severe exponents of the Spanish Inquisition seem jovial and tolerant. After much drink was taken, arguments about old resentments were unloaded.

If a farmer was disappointed with the price they got for the sheep they did not show it. I was never sure if their passive acceptance of bad news was born out of their faith or a sense of fatalism. Those living on a small farm were particularly vulnerable to the death of animals. If a few animals died, particularly cattle or calves, it decimated their paltry profits. The effects of such reversals were tangible. Christmas presents were smaller, new clothes were deferred a bit longer, old shoes remained in use, even when little holes began to appear in them.

A big social event for the local farmers was bringing the milk in horse and cart to the local creamery every day. As the farmers waited in the queue outside the creamery they shared local gossip before presenting the milk for testing. The more cream there was, the more money you got. Then they collected the skim milk at the back, which was used to feed the calves. The creamery was the very hub of the rural community.

In his wonderfully evocative play, *The Field*, John B. Keane, a chronicler of his time who offers an unforgettable evocation of his formative years, demonstrates that land is crucial to Irish people not just in economic terms but in terms of identity. My father's friends mostly owned small farms. The best way to unlock the secrets of their identities and personalities was to walk with them, in the softness of the western mist, through the fields, when the constant rain had left the world shimmering with droplets on every leaf. Our lives, just like those of all farmers, were ruled by the state of the rains and the light of the sun.

## *Wired for Sound*

An occasional feature of family life in Athlone was the retrieval of the dust-laden gramophone from its normal resting place under the bed. The first time I saw one I was thirteen and I thought it was a museum piece. It had a quaint old-world appearance and had to be wound up manually like a tin soldier. Although most people had about twenty gramophone records, the most popular was often Delia Murphy's 'Spinning Wheel'. Another particularly warm memory for me was the day my father brought home our first television set.

A few months earlier, a family of travellers had come to live a mile and a half away and been shunned by some of the local community. They were refused entry to some local pubs and shops. At Sunday Mass they sat together at the back of the church. None of the 'upright' pillars of the community would sit on the same seat as them. A few of the more superior parishioners decided to go to Mass in the neighbouring parish. I think about that incident every time I hear Christy Moore's song 'Go Move Shift' which parallels the original nativity story with the treatment of travellers.

The biggest crime of all was to be different. And yet the travelling community was in many ways very sophisticated, as was evident in the way they used language. It took real skill to disassemble the easy platitudes and decipher their real meaning. For example, speaking about a dead priest in rural Ireland was an artform which a PhD student in psycholinguistics would have found practically impossible. 'He was careful with money' meant that he was a reincarnation of Scrooge. On the other hand, 'Sure he had no interest in money' said that he had allowed the church and school to fall into rack and ruin. Worse still was: 'God bless him, the poor man put a lot of work into his sermons.' This was a dead giveaway. These sermons went on and on like a transatlantic ocean liner. The greatest depth of feeling was evident in an apparently casual remark – 'He didn't suffer fools gladly' – which revealed that nobody but nobody could get on with him. The poor priest just could not win.

I can still remember a time when I was young when our priest died. His funeral left an enduring imprint on me. There was genuine grief certainly, but what struck me forcefully was that nobody cried.

## To School Through the Streets

School days were not the happiest days of my life. I was particularly hostile to Irish grammar and only a few snippets of the language remained with me:

> '*Go mba leithsceal, a mhaistir.*' – 'Excuse me, sir.'
> '*Bhfuil gach duine ag eisteach?*' – 'Is everybody listening?'
> '*Gura mile maith agat.*' – 'Thanks very much.'
> '*Lamha sios!*' – 'Hands down!'
> '*Lamha suas!*' – 'Hands up!'

Learning catechism answers off by rote, for all my interest in religion, never constituted my idea of a good time – though, like so many of my generation, the questions and answers have remained enshrined in my brain:

> '*Who must your first love be?*'
> 'God.'
> '*And after God?*'
> 'Mary, my Mother in Heaven.'

41

Holiness at the time was virtually compulsory.

At school I was never a star student. No one would have picked me out as a girl who was going to do great things. My problem was not in being lazy but that I did not want to sit down and concentrate. I had too much dreaming to do. One of the few memorable moments came in a mathematics class when a pupil was asked what a cone was. The answer came immediately: 'An ice cream.'

Sr Mary Dympna stood head and shoulders above all other teachers. Like all good teachers she was firm, forthright and clear-headed. But she was also an extremely gentle and loving woman, with a soft streak of humanity, who inspired devotion among her pupils because of her charm, humour and reasonableness. Her almost unwrinkled brow was a plateau of piety. It was joked at the time that there were just four lessons you needed to become a teacher:

1. The history of Irish education was the hedge school.
2. Teaching methods – always, always, always use a blackboard.
3. School organisation – never build a school beside an open sewer or dung hill.
4. Educational psychology – make sure to get the pupil outside the classroom before they wet the floor.

Sr Mary Dympna's training was obviously much more expansive. Although I remember some of her words, I remember her passion more. Her genius as a teacher was that she was able to communicate and transmit this passion to her pupils and to awaken their creativity and take then on a magical journey of imaginative exploration, even if at times she took them on side-tracks because of the complexity of her language and the density and depth of her thought.

Her little asides were priceless gems; intimate, wry and chatty by turns, but always drawing her captive audience into moments of shared experience. What fascinated us all was her willingness to improvise, to experiment, to try something different. Our other teachers tried to pour the right answers into us, but she favoured stimulating us, helping us to see that there was generally more than one answer, but that we had to find them for themselves. She saw education as a form of archaeology, not about regurgitating old answers but digging for new ones. She loved words and her favourite expression could have been: 'Words must be weighed, not counted.'

Her pupils needed a hero or heroine, and her flair to inspire them with a different vision of life's possibilities was awesome. In the cloistered atmosphere of our stuffy classroom, our retiring teenage sensibilities were exposed to the full vigour of her powerful personality. Lively, highly intelligent, articulate, her thoughts exploded in a torrent of words and our minds raced to keep up. Her appearance was enhanced by her arresting dark eyes that sparkled, almost flashed, as ideas and indignation energised her mind. Her most frequent complaint was of the almost total lack of imagination in the classroom and that her pupils were living in a fog of uncertainty and ignorance.

No surprise then that I had Sr Mary Dymphna consecrate my two children after they were born.

Eternal life; I hardly knew what it meant until my teacher started to talk about it. I did not want to think about it and was pretty sure that I did not want it in my early years. All the bedtime stories I had heard in my youth finished with the words: 'And they all lived happily ever after.' Yet I acquired a contradictory image when I heard people complaining about 'an eternity of waiting' when they were fed up waiting for someone to serve them in a shop.

Sr Mary Dymphna filled my head with thoughts of a different God than the one I learned earlier. The first school image I had acquired of God was of an old man with a long flowing beard, dressed magisterially in white, having a leisurely chalice of whatever they drink 'up there' and reading heaven's equivalent of *The Irish Times*. This was the God who kept a little red book and entered all our sins on one side and our acts of goodness on the other side, like a spiritual ledger which determined whether I would be directed up or down on the celestial escalator on the last day.

Sr Mary Dymphna had stumbled on a different God, derived from her extensive reading of the works of the mystical writers like St John of the Cross. This was a God who dances and astonishes. The love of God had transported her, shattered her and consumed her like a fire. This was a passionate, heart-battering God, the God who swept her up to the heights in a blaze of flame, whose face was full of the beauty of all creatures, of incredible power and glory. Such was the beauty of God that we only partially taste it, like a dolphin dipping and plunging into the sea. I hoped heaven was the exciting place that Sr Mary Dymphna depicted.

The most influential people in anyone's life are the parents and the second most are their teachers. That is why teachers are so important. It is about making that difference.

## Rest in Peace

Although it sounds morbid, I always had a great fascination for wakes. Wakes had a peculiar function in Irish society – a mixture of the religious and the social. They were upstairs-downstairs situations with a difference.

Downstairs, the kitchen was a hive of activity: full of relatives and neighbours of the deceased. Men arrived in ones and twos. Bottles of stout, later whiskey, occasionally poteen, were distributed without any hesitation. Cigarettes and pipes gave out stifling swirls of smoke. Conversation became increasingly animated as the drink took its toll, with the price of cattle, the unsuitability of the weather for cutting the turf and the most recent football match important sources of conversation.

A black rosary beads threaded through the corpse's fingers. The air in the room was thick with silence. 'He was a decent man, God rest him. One of the old sort.' Outside the death room, the low hubbub of whispered speech offered a stark contrast to the eating and drinking. In the death room itself there was an almost hushed silence, especially as new sympathisers came in to kneel on the floor and say their few prayers and shake hands with the bereaved – silhouettes in the flickering candlelight. Soothing phrases were trotted out: 'One way or another, it will be the will of God.' The still corpse laid inevitably in the Franciscan-style brown habit, preparing to make the great reunion with their maker. The climax of the proceedings was always the saying of the Rosary before everybody left for home. A hush descended on the house until the chief mourner intoned the words:

'First, we'll offer the Holy Rosary up for the repose of his soul.'

'Thou O Lord wilt open my lips.'

'And my tongue shall announce Thy praise.'

'Lord have mercy,' they all said in unison at the end.

When the Rosary was said, the late callers placed their hands lightly over the hands of the deceased before leaving the room. It was believed at the time that if you did not touch the corpses they would haunt you.

## Good Neighbours
Neighbourliness was a powerful force in society. At no time was this more evident than at the Station Masses when huge crowds gathered

whenever the Mass was celebrated in someone's home. Each year the Stations appeared silently and suddenly, like the first snow.

Sharing between neighbours was commonplace at the time. If you were caught short of any essential item like tea or sugar your first thought was not to make the mile and a half journey to the local shop, but to ask the next-door neighbour. There was no shyness about making such a request. It was part of the natural order of things.

This was important for many women. They always made pounds of butter to give to their 'city cousins', by which they meant those who lived in towns like Athlone. Farming children always knew that Christmas was on its way when their mothers started baking Christmas cakes and puddings. The first clue that Christmas was coming was when they came home from school to see their mother with her sleeves rolled up to her elbows working energetically at the blue barrel butter churn.

## Changing Times

The anthem for the 1960s generation was: 'Hope I d-die before I get old.' Theirs was the generation which saw an unprecedented departure from previous generations. It was in the 1960s that life as we know it today was shaped and moulded. It was the decade of the Beatles, pirate radio, monster peace-concerts, flower power and Mary Quant. Hope and idealism were the common currency. Nostalgically everything about the time seems good, the concern for peace, the socially concerned songs of Bob Dylan and Joan Baez and the sense of freedom and optimism.

For a teenage girl in Athlone, one of the most significant transformations was the fashion revolution. Up to that point girls dressed like children until they were fifteen or sixteen and then, before they had time to draw their breath, they were given middle-aged clothes, like tweed suits. In the 1960s, for the first time, there were workable pretty clothes for teens and it was wonderfully liberating.

Higher educational standards, greater foreign travel, the Second Vatican Council brought the winds of change to Irish society. However, the greatest agent of social transformation was unquestionably the emergence of television when topics, which had hitherto been shrouded in a veil of secrecy, were openly discussed for the first time in Irish society. One programme in particular would have a dramatic impact.

And that was *The Late Late Show*. It's not just a television programme, it's a national institution – as was its first presenter, Gay Byrne. Since its inception in 1962, it had followed its commission to feature 'serious subjects and trivialities, small talk and big talk, bantering and blathering'. A proliferation of headline-grabbing episodes on lesbian nuns, unmarried mothers and most notably the saga of the bishop and the nightie had carved it a unique niche in Irish broadcasting. It was a conduit of social change, a communal confessional box and often great entertainment. Exposure on *The Late Late Show* was the ultimate dream for any publicist, because it was not simply a great platform it was *the* platform. Television was blamed for all manner of new social ills – typified in the late Oliver J. Flanagan's comment: 'There was no sex in Ireland before television.' Irish people became aware that they had a lot of catching up to do in many areas. One small example of this was Eamon de Valera's reaction to a visit to France: 'All I can say is that sex in Ireland is yet in its infancy!'

For the young me, these exciting changes were the sweetest music.

# 4

# Holy Mother

*'Let me not to the marriage of true minds*
*Admit impediments. Love is not love*
*Which alters when it alteration finds . . .'*

— WILLIAM SHAKESPEARE, 'Sonnet 116'

Catholicism cast a long shadow over all aspects of Irish society in the 1950s. There was a heavy wooden crucifix nailed up on a wall in most homes, flanked by pictures of sickly yellow and gloomy apostles. More saints and wounded martyrs watched over other rooms. Reading material consisted largely of religious magazines like *The Sacred Heart*, *The Far East* and *The Messenger* – although amongst the farming community *The Farmer's Journal* was their bible.

I had a particular reverence for Benediction. I loved the choir's singing, the air warm and heavy with incense and bodies and the tinkling of a bell. There always seemed to be a chorus of shrouded coughing coming from the pews from nervous parishioners, answering awkwardly to the priest's promptings. In silence and solemnity, the priest climbed towards the tabernacle. The monstrance glittering like a metallic sun as it moved it in the shape of a cross before a mass of adoring eyes. I marvelled at the altar boys, in scarlet and white, as they left the altar in twos in front of the priest bearing the empty monstrance, the light from the candles dancing daringly on the gold of his cloak.

Each year, like most Irish people at the time, I welcomed the fine weather by joining the rush to erect a May altar in honour of Our Lady. Boxes, tea chests and all kinds of idle implements were draped with white sheets to make homemade altars. Flowers were piled into jam jars for decorations.

I had a great love for the altar. I joined the Legion of Mary just so I could get up on the altar. I always suspected that if I touched the altar rail during the consecration I would get an electric shock.

During Lent, we often went without breakfasts. I have one very vivid memory of Lent. On one Ash Wednesday, Lily and I went to Mass but there was such a huge queue for ashes afterwards we didn't wait. When we got home we went to the range and got ashes from the range and put some on our foreheads. Petrified that we had committed a mortal sin, we confessed to the Canon.

From an early age I had a great love for the Virgin Mary, intercessor, mother of mercy, star of the sea. To call upon the Father for daily bread and to praise the kingdom, the power and the glory was inspiring and comforting. But I felt a warm glow within me when I spoke phrases like 'fruit of thy womb'.


*Mistletoe and Wine*

Like all children, I had a great love for Christmas and all the preparations for it. A big thrill was going to Dublin on the eighth of December. That was the day Dublin was invaded by the culchies for the serious business of Christmas shopping. This was not as easy as it sounded, as all the better-off people in rural Ireland had congregated in Dublin for the same purpose and all had targeted the prestigious shops like Clerys to make their purchases. The shop doors were continually opening, with the steady flow of bargain hunters, though some were there only to browse. There was barely room to sneeze.

People travelled by train from Athlone in the morning darkness, an event in itself, with the stops in all the little towns and the commuters coming and going like buzzing bees, the struts, smoke and sparks as the powerful engine clickety-clacked to the capital city. The lucky ones grabbed the window seat and marvelled at the flashing world as the sky got lighter until it was broad daylight. This was something special, like a trip to fairyland, a glorious treat that would repay all the weeks of being good. The enduring image was always of the Christmas lights. The simplicity of the lights was in stark contrast to the hive of activity and crazy traffic in the 'big smoke'.

Scurrying shoppers like ants at a party, arms laden with gift-wrapped Christmas presents headed home as the Dublin dusk descended. A little girl was mesmerised by Switzers' window with its glorious gnomes, who moved majestically to the rhythm of the music. Crowds gathered, young and old, just to savour the innocence of it all.

Christmas back then really began in earnest on 'Big Saturday', the Saturday before the holiday, when we journeyed into town to 'bring home the Christmas'. It was far and away the busiest day of the year in the town, a fascinating mixture of the festive spirit and hard-nosed business.

The market square in Athlone was buzzing with the 'making of the deal', an event which inevitably provoked heated argument, exaggerated claims and affected disinterest and which ended either in stubborn resistance or with warm handshakes and 'Gawd Bless you, Mam, and a happy Christmas to you and yours'. The three items sold on the square were geese, turkeys and Christmas trees. The trees were subjected to intense scrutiny: all trees had to be the genuine article, the faintest suggestion of anything artificial was regarded as nothing less than sacrilege.

There was the obligatory excursion to the friary for Mass preceded by confession, for which everyone queued interminably. On the window ledges huge, white candles flickered slightly as a draught touched them, then shone as brightly as before. Despite the solemnity of the Mass, the incense smelled more beautiful than a springtime primrose.

The main shops were then visited. The prices of the most important items were carefully collated, before necessities as well as luxuries were purchased, stretching family financial resources to the very limit. A high level of skill was needed to fit all the ingredients for the Christmas feast into the boot of the car. Tins of biscuits were a rare treat for most families. Every good customer in the local post office-cum-grocer-cum-newsagent got a tin of biscuits and a calendar. It was a gesture of appreciation for patronage during the year.

The highlight of the day for the children was a visit to the biggest shop in town to see Santa Claus. The toyshop was like an Aladdin's cave to my spellbound eyes. Children always loved the way the little bell went 'ching' as they opened the door. Armed with a shining two-shilling piece, the requisite fee for the honour of being received by Santa, we took our place in the queue in a state of high excitement.

The huge shop windows displaying their wares for all prospective buyers to see: sweets, toffees, chocolates and cakes of every brand and colour. The intoxicating smell of freshly baked bread drew me to the shop where cream cakes were stacked enticingly on cluttered glass shelves. Lorries thundered down the narrow Connacht Street.

Men eyed the pubs with relish, suddenly conscious of a terrible thirst.

The Sunday before Christmas was always the day for setting up the crib. This task was conducted with an air of great solemnity. The shepherds and the angels, the ox and the ass had all been carefully wrapped in old newspaper to preserve their bright colours. All this was carefully stored in a box in the attic or in the outside shed. In our house, a winding staircase led up through what appeared as an extraneous round tower and there was the most fantastic collection of bric-à-brac and memorabilia collected during my father's lifetime. Dust and debris were everywhere, only stirred from year to year by a rat's foot or looting mice. The task was normally rushed to make sure we didn't miss a second of *the* undisputed most popular programme in rural Ireland *The Riordans*.

The crib gave me an agonising insight into the minds and hearts of the characters of the first Christmas. The story was old yet new each year. Children never failed to wonder at the wonderful, how God took time to enter human history. The baby's life was one of contradiction even at birth because a young girl, still a virgin, gave him life. His birth was so significant that, that evening, the stars were thrown into rapture and subservience. An infant's voice was turning the world on its head. He was only different in seeing evil, but not being it.

It was easy for me to feel a particular sympathy for Mary. I felt a kinship with her because we were both born into a very rigid and traditional society. Such a close-knit community had advantages and disadvantages. The major disadvantage is that there is no way of maintaining one's privacy. News of Mary's 'shame' must have been music to the ears of all the gossips, and Israel's local gossips had many equivalents in Athlone. It was not difficult to imagine how painful it must have been for Mary to know that everyone was talking about her. In the Jewish society of that time, like Athlone in mine, doing the right thing was less important than being seen to do the right thing. For this reason, I was able to make connections between the first Christmas story and my own.

I understood how painful and distressing it must have been for Mary to see Joseph, the man to whom she was betrothed, become another innocent victim of this gossip as well. I could only imagine what it must have been like for Mary to have set off on a long journey on the back of a donkey. Having seen people travelling on the back of a donkey myself, I had a good inkling as to what was involved for her. Worse was to follow. There was no place where she could have her baby even in meagre comfort. Then, after having her baby, she had to flee the stable because somebody wanted to kill her child.

When the Magi brought gifts to the babe in the manger they invented the art of giving presents at Christmas. I noted the significance of Christ coming as the greatest gift of all, but also as one receiving gifts. This suggested that love is about receiving as well as giving. To have one without the other diminishes its power and leaves a gap in the lives of those who wish to participate in it. This was a welcome corrective to the warped understanding of Christian love my parents' generation had assimilated, as something we 'do' for others. The enormity of meaning in the incarnation is almost mind-blowing, yet the crib did help us children to understand a simple, but profound truth. Jesus came and made himself small, so that we could be raised to heights we could not dared to have dreamed of otherwise.

During the last few days at school before the Christmas holidays our normal timetable of maths, Irish, English, history and geography was suspended. A lot of new Christmas carols were learned. There were lines from individual carols which penetrated the brain, highlighting the catechetical value of these songs. A line that struck the class most forcibly was one from 'The Little Drummer Boy': '. . . and he smiled at me.' The idea that Jesus was smiling at us stressed our dignity and value in God's eyes more eloquently than any sermon could have done. It was a warm message.

Two lines from 'Little Town' also set us thinking.

> *How silently, how silently,*
> *the wondrous gift is given.*

The image of God portrayed in these lyrics was of a shy God; not someone who wanted to be in the limelight but someone who was more comfortable in the background. Somehow we found that an attractive quality. The mood of 'Joy to the World' was very inspiring and evocative. The picture that came to our minds listening to that song was of a dancing God, rejoicing at the happiness of humankind, even it was only a temporary affair.

## *Joy to the World*

Some old customs could momentarily transfigure our existence and let the eternal shine through. One such custom was the singing of carols. They also struck us as simple ways of expressing those parts of Christianity that ordinary people found most interesting, not the parts that people ought to find most interesting. They were memorable because they were so tangible. They celebrated things that we could touch and see and warm to: a mother and a baby, though curiously not a father, or at least not a real father, a stable, donkeys, shepherds, straw and hay. The miracle they celebrated was the making of an all-powerful God, child-sized, so that even the youngest infant could grasp what it was all about. More importantly, they reminded us of the happy character of our faith, that Christianity was a reason for rejoicing. God became small for the sole purpose of saving us all. This was part of the beauty of the festive season where past and future meet in the present.

Learning these carols did have a practical value for students of the time because they could sing them on Wren Day. On St Stephen's Day, the 26th of December, young boys and men dressed up in old clothes, painted their faces and cycled to all the houses for miles around, where they sang, or more often wailed, in the confident expectation that they could be rewarded with a few coins for their musical offering. Motley groups appeared on the roads or laneways dressed in their assorted costumes, including straw hats and faces masked or painted. They did a jig or reel or sang a traditional song, trying to disguise their voices, clinking the coins in their collection tins, chorused their thanks and were on the way to make more money. Their motivation was purely mercenary, but the carols did help us in a small way to comprehend a mystery they could only dimly understand.

## Keep Them Busy

In school, many pupils were 'encouraged' to incorporate an inspirational or religious message in their recitation for the day. The messages 'suggested' included some religious poems which went over our heads! The message 'suggested' for many was the St John of the Cross poem 'The Incarnation':

*Then He called*
*The archangel Gabriel*
*And sent him to*
*The Virgin Mary*

*At whose consent*
*The mystery was wrought*
*In whom the Trinity*
*Clothed the Word with flesh*

*And though Three work this*
*It is wrought in the One;*
*And the Word lived incarnate*
*In the womb of Mary.*

*And He who had only a father*
*Now had a Mother too,*
*But she was not like others*
*Who conceive by man.*

*From her own flesh*
*He received His flesh*
*So he is called*
*Son of God and of man.*

At school, we also learned many favourite Christmas stories. One was the story of how Christmas stopped a war when the fierce and bloody First World War came to a temporary halt on the day of Christ's birth in one corner of the Western Front. The Germans waved and called out in simple French, holding out cigars as they asked for English jam in return. '*Stille Nacht*' and 'Silent Night' rang out on different sides. The languages were different, but the sentiments remained the same. A ball was produced and a football match took place. Music and sport, two of the languages which could have united the participants at the tower of Babel.

The 24th was the day when families finished their four thousand Hail Marys, which they begun on the first day of Advent. These prayers were to be said in honour of the four thousand years the Jews waited for the coming of the Messiah.

Some years the local priest called to the school and patiently explained that not everyone enjoys Christmas, particularly those who are lonely or those who have no money to buy 'nice things' for Christmas. Those of us who were the lucky ones had a special obligation to 'bring Christmas' to those who were not so fortunate. The priest often quoted Thomas Merton who wrote: 'With those for whom there is no room is Jesus.' He went on to say:

'I like to think also that especially at Christmas, with those for whom there is no one to share their rooms is Jesus. The sad reality is that life is difficult for many people. The message of Christmas is that Christ is made flesh not in the unreal beauty of the Christmas card, but in the mess that is our world. For those of us who claim to be Christian, Christ is made flesh in our neighbours. The true meaning of Christmas is that God so loved the world that he sent his only son to save us.'

On Christmas Eve, in most Irish homes, the curtains were stripped off the windows and a single candle was put to burn in each sill till the morning. In many cases the back door remained unlocked whatever the weather, so that there was no danger of Mary and Joseph going astray in their search for a resting place. Across the fields houses glittered, the light from their candles like jewelled pin-points in the darkness.

Torn by longings I was unable to assuage, I was incapable of settling. Anticipation was always the keenest pleasure. Bursting with impatience, I resolved to stay awake all night, to sneak a peep through the bannister, to catch a glimpse of Santa's red cloak. The stockings were not to be touched until after the Christmas dinner. Then the presents were pulled out and examined with squeaks of delight and excitement. I always thought it was a strange custom that children should hang up stockings, but no matter how hard I tried I could never find any adult I knew who would explain it to me. I understood their reticence when I discovered that the idea sprung from St Nicholas saving three beautiful sisters from a life of prostitution. He gave anonymous gifts of gold for their dowries by throwing bags of money through the windows while the young women slept, and into the stockings which were hanging ready for the morning.

On Christmas mornings, I woke early, long before the first faint vestiges of light illuminated the specklings of frost on the hard ground. I rushed downstairs with my brothers, drawn as if by a magnet to the place under the Christmas tree, where hopefully Santa Claus had neatly piled our presents. Competition was intense as to who was to be the first to make the discovery, to shriek out: 'He came, He came!' Our excitement transmitting like electricity; our shining faces a fitting reward to the idea of Santa.

At Mass that morning there was always a crush of people. The attendance was swelled by people who had returned home for Christmas, a welcome respite for families divided by economic necessity. Christmas Eve was a time of delirious reunions as trains and buses to Athlone brought husbands, fathers, daughters, sons, girlfriends and boyfriends home to the bosom of their families. The standard greeting of Mass-goers to one another was 'A Happy Christmas', though some went native and said, '*Go mberimid beó ag an am seo arís*', their breath like plumed smoke in the frosty air. Inside, the focal point was the crib, with a big silver star shining in the roof, and a little baby so real I would not have been surprised if he began to wail in his diminutive straw manger. It did at least remind me that it was a baby, not Santa Claus that was, is and always would be, Christmas.

The priest wore his best gold and white embroidered vestments, and the pale wax candles on the altar gleamed amid the lilies and greenery. The final candle in the advent wreath was lit ceremoniously. So many of my images of Christ are etched in light, the silver of frost and moonlight, the shining Star of Bethlehem guarding the Magi and the radiance of the lighted candles.

The choir sang lustily, the leader in his deep, booming, nasal voice intoned the *Credo in unum De–e–um*, whereupon the bright sparks in the congregation, with a few words of Latin, chimed in respectfully with '*Pa-c-trem Omninpotentem*', or words to that effect. Then the leading female singer gave a solo rendering of 'O Holy Night' that was so beautiful it worked a minor miracle and hushed all the coughing and shuffling. The *pièce de résistance* was her solo version of '*Adestes Fideles*'.

The gospel was taken from Saint Luke and began: 'In the sixth month, the angel Gabriel was sent from God to the city of Galilee named Nazareth to a virgin betrothed to a man named Joseph.'

I was always enthralled by the idea of angels. The pictures I saw of angels were of creatures robed in white with outspread wings, kindly smiles and celestial vision. Angels were always good but essentially heavenly. I liked them because they formed a tenuous connection between the unseen worlds and signified the greatest of mysteries, humankind's passage through time.

Like many people, from my earliest moments, the spirit of Christmas for me has centred around the family. Lucky enough to have a relatively prosperous family life, I was keenly aware of the less fortunate and conscious of my own good fortune. The contrasts are most stark at Christmastime, particularly in relation to money and privilege. It was also a hectic, busy time, with all the family caught up in the preparations. Christ was coming, a list of presents had to be drawn up. It is a time for memories – blushes at the memory of nights trying to stay awake to see or catch the red-coated figure with his sack, baking cakes and church bells beating the air were all part of the build-up.

Our family were very traditional. The spirit of Christmas was all wrapped up in the traditional things like big roaring fires, Christmas trees, tinsel, hot ports. These embodied the good feelings of the festive season – friendship, warmth, a time to forget old grudges, a time for family and friends to come together, even people who normally don't talk to each other.

Culinary innovation was not a feature of my childhood. Then one year my mother caused a major shock when she produced Brussels sprouts for Christmas dinner. It was the first time any of us had ever seen them. My father looked at them for a long time and poked them around his plate for what seemed like an eternity with a disdainful look on his face. We waited his verdict with bated breath. Eventually he asked, 'Who made a balls of the cabbage?'

A particular joy for those, like me, with younger brothers and sisters was watching their faces as they opened their presents. Another favourite was feeling my own presents, trying to guess what was in them without actually opening them. It was a time for fun and for letting my hair down, but above all a time for giving, especially to those who were closest to me. The time after Christmas day was also special. Things had quietened down at that stage and people were more relaxed, with time to call on friends and distant family.

Looking back, I remember the Christmases of my childhood with great affection because they nurtured my understanding of the season, which remains with me to this day, as a time of mystery, magic, hope and above all innocence.

## Man of Distinction

The town of Athlone has many famous sons and daughters, notably Count John McCormack, a man who bestrode the musical world like a colossus in the early part of the twentieth century. He, too, was a big part of my childhood. Years later it produced a man who would leave a huge impression on the Irish political landscape: Dr Noel Browne. Born in 1914, the son of a former policeman in the RIC, he lived his early life under the black shadows of tuberculosis – his father was the first who died from the disease in his family, to be followed by his mother, a brother and sister when the family moved to London.

Thanks to the generosity of a family friend he was able to study in the hallowed Trinity College Dublin, where he qualified as a doctor. Shortly afterwards he fell victim of the disease itself. When he recovered he dedicated his life to eradicating this blight on Irish life.

This pernicious disease, which had already eroded Ireland's diminishing population for generation after generation, was killing between three thousand and four thousand people every year. Through the imaginative introduction of the Hospitals' Sweepstake Scheme, funding was provided to remedy the main deficiency in the treatment of TB patients – a shortage of beds – and sanatoria were provided to deal with the epidemic. The new sanatoria coincided with important medical advances such as the introduction of BCG and the use of streptomycin. Not only cure but prevention became possible because of the combination of mass radiography, sanatoria, modern methods of treatment and vaccination.

Life in the sanatorium was bleak. The only colour in this pebble-dash world was the people. The nurses were generally gentle and sympathetic, noted for their warmth and infinite kindness as for their gritty honesty and dog-like devotion, although on occasions there were some who, because of over work or lack of sleep, were on a short fuse.


## The Smiling Statue

Tuberculosis was still a real killer at the time, and I was to discover its agonies at first hand.

In the 1950s, I got a shadow on my lung and was in real danger of death. My faith kept me going and I made my first Communion when I had TB. I remember I had a great love for St Teresa. A song came out called 'St Teresa of the Roses', which fuelled my devotion to her. I had a feeling of great closeness with her. There was never a second I felt completely alone, though I was often lonely.

Then, when I was at my lowest, there was to be a dramatic divine intervention.

My mother thought I was going to die. I was physically in a very bad way and lying in my bed at home when the statue of Our Lady turned and smiled at me. The memory of that smile would sustain me, because I was to have a lot of suffering, physical and emotional, in the weeks and months ahead.

My condition deteriorated to such an extent that I was sent to a sanatorium in Dublin. The expectation was that once you were sent there the only way you came out of that place was in a coffin.

My father and mother came as often as they could to see me, but they had no car at the time so they had to travel by bus. Daddy would read the books of Blessed Martin de Porres to me. Although in some ways I had everything I ever wanted, I was a bit disappointed that I was apparently forgotten by my school friends. When I was in high infants, a nun made up a lovely parcel for a friend when she had TB. It hurt me when they didn't do the same for me.

That was relatively minor, though, by comparison with some of my other problems. I really dreaded every day in the hospital. One day I refused to eat the gristle which was to be our main meal. The sister held my nose and made me eat it. I got sick and threw it all up again. Then she made me clean up the mess.

I was always afraid of nurses because I used to wet the bed. Although there was one beautiful young nurse, the others gave out a lot to me. One time my aunt sent me flowers. One of the nurses gave them to one of the other girls in the ward. When I said they were mine she said, 'Don't be cheeky.' However, I was even more afraid of one of the patients who made my life a total misery. She was an awful bully. Once when I got a gift of five shillings, which was a lot of money in those days, she made me give her half of it. In this climate of fear I felt unloved.

That girl who bullied me hit me harder than the TB.

Then, completely out of the blue, I was cured. The shadow just disappeared from my lung. My father always claimed that it was Our Lady who cured me. As a gesture of thanks he arranged the building of a grotto to Our Lady of Lourdes in Athlone. I will never forget the day I left the sanatorium. It was like getting out of jail. I was so happy until I heard that my uncle Jack died during my time in the sanatorium.

### *Nine to Five*

I remember the time after my cure from TB as a time of great love. I regularly had to go Mullingar for X-rays. My aunt used to bring me in the ambulance. She bought me my first tricycle and beautiful clothes and jewellery. I went back to England with her and went to school in Fulham – starting in eighth grade. Every year I went over for six months. Separation from my family at home was hard. As I was the first child it was hard for my parents, too. I was their guinea pig, in a sense. I know that parenting is a learning process. Sometimes it's difficult to know if you are doing right or wrong for your child.

School days were far from the happiest days of my life. Even so, I loved sewing and cookery. They were real. I was never interested in a career. I just wanted to be married. My biggest problem, though, was that I never had the figure I wanted. This gave me a terrible inferiority complex. I always felt that everyone was better than me even when they weren't.

When the bishop made me a strong and perfect Christian at my Confirmation the responsibility weighed lightly on my shoulders. I was more interested in my new outfit. I was lucky in that my parents could afford a new outfit for me. It was the convention of the time that, because of economic necessity, clothes and footwear were bought a few sizes too large. An outfit was meant to last longer than just one day and eventually be passed on to a younger brother or sister. Not so for my Confirmation dress. I remember, Confirmation was one of the few highpoints of my schooldays.

I did my primary cert and left school when I was only fourteen.

I worked in a factory, now known as Elan, making pressure gauges for a Danish company. Then I went to Casey's shop in town, serving at the counter and selling wallpaper. I loved meeting people. After that I went to England to my aunt and uncle. I went to work in a restaurant in Twickenham, where the hours were very long. I loved the clothes, especially the minis, but I missed out on the decadence of the swinging sixties as I had to be in by half-nine.

Then, when I was sixteen, I came home again. I got a job in the Gentex factory. At first, I got a hard time there because some people said I didn't need a job as my parents had a shop. Once I got over that I loved the place, but it closed down so I had to start from scratch again.

In my teenage years I didn't know what it was like to go out with the girls. I did the housework and the shopping. The saddest part of my life was that because my mother worked so hard, I never really got the chance to be with her. When I started going to dances I at least had a chance to talk with my father like an adult. I told him who I met and who I talked to. Things changed later when I got married. I was no longer a McCormack, I was a Carroll.

The great love of my life during my teenage years was Elvis Presley. I had pictures of Elvis all over the walls with the picture of the Sacred Heart in the centre. I even had a picture of Elvis on the ceiling. When I was young I was shifted to another room for a short while when an uncle came home from America. On his first night in the house he let out an awful scream. He though a ghost was coming down to haunt him – but it was only my picture of Elvis!

## Rome Changes Everything

In 1958 the Catholic Church underwent a major shift when the son of an Italian peasant became Pope John XXIII. The smiling pope realised that the Church was standing still in the middle of a changing world. In 1960 he announced his decision to call the Second Vatican Council. In 1962 Pope John XXIII brought the bishops of the Church together to meet him in Rome, the first time this had been done in nearly a century. His aim was to rescue the faith that had got lost in rules and practices and addiction to power.

It is not simply important but vital to adequately appreciate the realities of life before that Second Council to understand the wider context. To contemporary eyes, some of the practices of the time almost defy belief, but we must make our understanding of the period critically appropriate by trying to look through the lens of that time not our own. Salvation then was attained by rejecting and shunning the worldly dimension of our human existence. This existence itself was often seen as sinful and unworthy, and the emphasis was on the salvation of one's soul which would be attained in the next life. There was a risk that the ecclesiastical apparatus of the Church might overshadow the action of the Holy Spirit and of grace in people's lives. The shadow of the 'temptation to Pharisaism', a deep attachment to habitual forms of religious expression rather than to the spirit of life they aimed to express, hovered ominously. Inside the system of the Pharisees was a quest for legal purity, going from one subtlety to another and ending in narrow legalism that our Lord fought against.

Pope John XXIII went on to suggest that the Church needed to reform and deepen its own vision of the Church. This was not the task of one single person, the sovereign pontiff or a certain number of cardinals, but the task of the entire Catholic world. New ideas and movements would arise in response to local and regional opportunities and they needed the freedom to develop and the approval of the authorities.

The Second Vatican Council made many changes in the way the Catholic Church operated and whole systems of thought unfurled. The winds of change were blowing, but the changes were not to everybody's taste. Many of them, like replacing the Latin Mass with the vernacular, were external. The root and branch reform which the Council had envisaged caused more profound reverberations. The wide-ranging changes in the Church mirrored deep changes in society. Christians could not but be affected by the radical developments in society around them, as well as the changes in the Church. Changes in educational status were also important. Before the Council, the clergy were the educated class in the Church. In the new situation, the laity were sometimes more theologically competent than the clergy.

Once free education was introduced in the late 1960s, people were no longer prepared to blindly obey the Church. Free education meant that the majority of people were questioning their faith for the first time. The best way to sum up the change was that there was a switch from the experience of authority to the authority of experience.

The effects of the Council were profound for the priests and nuns in particular. Up until then their lives were very monastic, which saw them living in 'cells' and with little freedom for individuality. When they entered those monastic lives, they believed they had left home for ever and many of them will have missed their parents.

Expressing one's own ideas and independence guaranteed getting into trouble. Two Sisters I know away at college wanted to return to their home convent for the funeral of a beloved colleague. The only way they could do this was by thumbing a lift and they felt that they had to remove their veils to do so. Unfortunately, they were spotted and the news spread to the convent and when they got back in the door they were immediately told that they were in 'very big trouble'.

Young Sisters were often presented with the ideal of having to be 'perfect' and to be very hard on and very critical of themselves. On a weekly basis the communities gathered confessed their failings individually in front of one another, each beginning with the words: 'Mother I confess...' during the Chapter of Faults. Sisters were literally given a stick, known as 'The Discipline', to beat themselves with, and often did so by getting into a rhythm, chanting the *Miserere*. If you had a false start you did it again. The harder they hit themselves the better for their souls. This beating was an integral part of religious life and seen as perfectly normal in the culture of the time. Mortification of the body was part of the route to perfection.

During Holy Week, Sisters ate breakfast standing up and sat on the ground for dinner. Before a Sister made their Profession, the youngest in the novitiate could boss them around for the day to help them learn obedience. These Sisters were not served meals for a day. Rather, to help them learn the meaning of poverty, they had to go around the refectory with their plate asking colleagues for food.

A tangible sign of the desire of all religious congregations to keep their Sisters from being 'tainted' by lay people was the 'Nuns' Room' in University College Cork (UCC), where Sisters from all the congregations went during breaks between lectures. Moreover, to ensure that clerics and religious literally did not drink the soup of secularism, a big long table was set up at lunch time in UCC exclusively for Sisters and seminarians so that they would not be 'contaminated' by lay people.

Obedience was to the Mother Superior and her biases and prejudices ruled supreme. To take one example: after Christmas dinner in one of the convents in Athlone the Mother Superior graciously passed around a box of sweets and instructed, 'Take plenty. Take two.'

Increasingly, however, the old ways felt like a song sung out of tune. Vatican II opened up a new understanding of mission, mystery and community. A big challenge was to keep the balance between these three – and to do so with joy. Mission awareness included the recognition that the Sisters were on both an inner and an outer journey, crossing the threshold into the sacred space.

Before Vatican II, the Sisters lived a very regimented life which left nothing to their own discretion, but the coming years would see incremental relaxation of the old rigidities. In practical terms, for example, it became no longer necessary to get permission to go to the dentist. For all Sisters, the first time they were given their own key to the convent was a moment of great liberation. Some of the changes were evident to all, such as the ending of practices like kneeling to kiss the floor and the long-awaited demise of the Chapter of Faults.

As the scale of the new challenges facing them became ever more apparent, some map or guide was clearly needed to navigate Catholics on their journey – and they were prepared to forgo the seduction of safety. It required courage to shift their perception of things, to transform their consciousness of the mystery that they were. The Church listened to an inborn whisper, because they prayed extensively. They recognised that if they continued to do what they had always done, they would continue to get what they had always got.

The Church felt the call to reach out with empathy to those in agony, as Jesus had done nearly two thousand years before, so that they could give adequate witness to the suffering Christ, who never failed to show extraordinary tenderness to the damaged, the despairing and the distressed.

In the Gospels we found Jesus repeating over and over again the simple advice: 'Watch and pray.' This was not merely a readiness for unexpected death. Its scope is far wider than that. It is to be alert to the call of God in one's immediate situation. As the old tree of established structures was dying, it was not easy to discern how to graft anew to the future vine. The Church found itself at an in-between time in its history: caught between a rich tradition and an as yet unformed new direction – a process that raised fears as well as bringing new promise.

There was less 'traditional' religion and more God in these gatherings of substance and spirit. There were minor moments of epiphany which beckoned beyond the here and now, into something immense at times of a widespread breakdown of trust in established institutions and a searching for alternatives, some of them extreme. There was a greater awareness that Jesus did not expect Christians to save the whole world; that was and is His job – but their homework every day was to try and help one neighbour at a time. In the later words of Pope Francis, to be shepherds who 'smell of the sheep'.

There was a new emphasis on joy. St Teresa of Avila's prayer was invoked: 'God deliver us from sorrow-filled saints.'

There was a new emphasis on Good News – though from time to time, some people had to be reminded that if they believed in the Good News they really needed to tell that to their faces.

I, though, had a big smile on my face for a very different reason.

I was in love.

Truly, madly deeply.

# 5

# Love Is All Around Me

*'Tire not of new beginnings . . .*
*build thy life — never upon regret*
*always upon resolve!*
*shed no tear on the blotted*
*page of the past*
*but turn the leaf and smile . . .*
*to see the clean white virgin page before thee.'*

— CARDINAL O'CONNELL, *Selected Homilies*

The happiest day of my life was the fifth of June 1972, the day I married the love of my life. Up to then, I was a young, vivacious girl with many admirers, especially a young man from Cork, but I had never loved a man before Jimmy. Up until then there had merely been coy looks, flirtatious chatter and sweet smiles. Actions more risqué could not be contemplated in the climate of the times, especially with my father keeping a keen eye out for anything that might transgress the clearly defined boundaries of acceptable behaviour of a Catholic girl.

I was told the facts of life when I was thirteen. My parents told me that I was not to become pregnant until I got married, but if I ever did to be sure and come back to them no matter what.

In rural and small-town Ireland, feminism seemed an impossible dream in the late 1960s. A girl was treated as a child until she was at least sixteen and then, on leaving school, she would be expected to clean, wash and darn at her parents' home until a man with an appropriate income came to ask for her hand in marriage. Except for those bold few who dared to dream of attending university and thought in terms of a career, a woman's late teens, even for those working in shops or in factories, were spent learning how to become a housewife.

Many Irish parents still had not caught up with the mood of the swinging sixties and continued to expect their daughters not to speak to a boy unless they were actually introduced to him. On dates, young people were expected to behave in a way the local parish priest would approve of. These traditional values seemed strangely out of place in a world that was frantically trying to rid itself of 'Victorian values'. Many parents did not like the new air of informality. They were determined that, in their family, at least, the old values of honesty, courtesy and allegiance to Catholicism would be upheld.

This moral code was rigid and tended to be enforced quite severely – demanding unquestioning obedience and strict adherence to the letter of the law. It provoked a multitude of reactions from teenagers and young adults varying from wilful disobedience to respectful conformism. At the end of the 1960s, the tension between old and new was clearly evident in Athlone as it was in most Irish towns.

Teenage relationships, a new term, in the 1960s, were still very innocent, unaffected by commercial pressure to couple up and become 'sexually active'. The fact that the most daring thing a teenager could say was that someone was 'a bit of all right' typified the teeming innocence of the time. Since the overwhelming majority of Irish young people still went to Sunday Mass, there was a moral foundation for remaining chaste, but the biggest fear was for a girl to get 'in the family way', or more usually 'in trouble', which almost inevitably meant an early marriage. Teenagers who went 'all the way' were generally considered by their peers to be a bit fast and not 'nice'. The older generation would ostracise them completely.

The 'nicer' teenagers believed in socialising as a group rather than pairing off for intimate moments. There were not the opportunities in Athlone to go to many different places other than the Ritz cinema or a dance. Girls were taught never to let a boy 'have his way' with them. Boys were taught that it was not nice to go out with one girl after another and that you should never take advantage of anyone. Those who steadfastly refused to blaspheme, smoke, drink or argue back with their parents seemed to their contemporaries to be a little old-fashioned but, to their parents, they were exactly what was expected.

The dance halls of the time served nothing other than minerals and bags of crisps. They were the setting for many rites of passages. Some of the girls danced together – steps rehearsed at home or in school corridors. The fellas with a bellyful of porter did circles asking every girl in the hall for a dance with a spectacular lack of success. In the slippery toilets, nervous young men combed their hair. The arms of their more confident friends rested around a girl's shoulder. Young women headed into the toilets in droves. Both young men and women had planned their strategy in advance and rated each prospective venue for 'talent'. Although the newspapers in the late 1960s were full of Vietnam, Martin Luther King and the civil rights struggle in America, the civil war in Biafra, the ferment in the Middle East after the Lightning War between Israel and her three Arab neighbours Egypt, Jordan and Syria, and closer to home, the escalating sectarian tension which preceded the civil rights demonstrations in Northern Ireland the following year, the talk in the dance hall was, as always, about local news.

Conversation was on the lines of:

'Did you get off with that girl in blue last week?' 'No such luck.'

'Mary and Jim have broken up again.' 'But sure they were made for each other.'

I was full of confidence in a group but tongue-tied when left alone with the boy I fancied. In my teenage years I often found my face burning with unpredictable blushes.

Love was to change all that.

## No Dancing Queen

Star of *Strictly Come Dancing* I am not. Yet I did have my moments on the dance floor, even if I dazzled few young men with my twinkle toes or smooth moves!

I had gladly left school for the promise of freedom bought with a working woman's wage. A combination of chance occurrences led me to my future husband. I can remember the day when I met my husband-to-be as if it were yesterday.

I met him on the sixth of December 1970 at a dance with the worst band in Ireland. I had been dancing with an English man, who was not very nice and I couldn't wait to be away from him, when I tripped over someone's foot. The first thing I noticed was that he was wearing a beautiful suit, and that he had a gorgeous smile and red hair. He asked me to dance and then if he could stay for the next one. I asked him 'Can you waltz?' He said, 'I don't know but I'll try.' He bought me a mineral. When the dance was over he asked if he could walk me home. I said yes, but on the way warned him that he wasn't to try anything because I wasn't that sort of girl. We agreed to meet the following Tuesday at eight p.m.

My parents gave me my values. They always said that if the boy thinks enough of you he would collect you at your house. I took a half-day on the Tuesday so that I could get ready. I was ready long before eight. I looked out the window, but still I kept him waiting a quarter of an hour.

Jimmy had been going out with a girl from Banagher when we met. He had to break it off, but I had the agony of wondering if he would go back to her. We were going out together for a short time when he brought me to my first dinner dance. I remember wearing a black dress and being nervous because I had never been at anything like it before. My mother told me to watch the crowd and do what they were doing.

We went to our second dinner dance on the sixth of February 1971. I thought he was going to dump me when he put his coat on my shoulders and I knew he had something out of the ordinary to say. He said he would love to be married to me and I said I would love to be engaged.

We had to delay our engagement for a while until Jimmy got his holiday pay to buy the ring. Eventually we went to Sheffield's jewellers to make the purchase. The ring we chose cost twenty-seven pounds. I left him alone in the shop to pay for it. I was embarrassed, afraid he wouldn't have the money. We got officially engaged on the fifth of June 1971. That night I put my arm around him in a way that everyone could see the ring.

I can still see Jimmy that first night I met him. Despite his beautiful smile I didn't fall for him because of his looks. There was something special inside him and in all the years since I've never doubted that he was made of the right stuff. Every day I hear about people falling in love, but I always believed that our love was very special and went beyond the normal. Something deep within me told me that Jimmy was the man I wanted to spend my life with. It was such a fantastic feeling to know that someone loved you so completely. Things were made easier because of the fact that all my family loved Jimmy as well. My father had always said that whoever asked me for my hand in marriage would have to ask him first. So one night when we were all out together Jimmy followed him into the gents and that obstacle was overcome without any difficulty. Nobody was saying *what are you rushing for* because they all knew we were madly in love.

## The Chapel of Love

Weddings were an unusual phenomenon in rural Ireland. They caused many a bitter feud between families, but sometimes were used to heal long drawn-out hostilities. Unmerciful rows were sparked off when people who thought they should have been invited to the wedding, but were not, vented their spleen in the most forceful way possible. Every past indiscretion or mistake, real or imagined, not only of the family in question, but of three previous generations of that family would be raked over the ashes. Inevitably a cold war broke out between the two families, which might take years to resolve and sometimes was never resolved. On the other hand, families who had fallen out – the most common cause of such hostilities was a failure to keep up fences on farms – might use an invitation to a wedding as a way of mending the fences in their relationship if not the actual ditches themselves.

An incident with the seating arrangements had been far too public for my father's liking, but not even that spoiled the day for him or for anyone else. There is a particular code, which applies to the description of weddings in the west of Ireland. The meaning is always hidden by the words. Rarely is the direct criticism pursued though the viciousness, and it can be all the more striking because of that. 'T'was a good job I had a feed before I left,' or worse still, 'If there were any mice there they would have starved with the hunger.' A 'great' wedding meant a good wedding. The ultimate derogatory comment was a 'nice' wedding, which was a disguised way of saying it was deadly boring.

For the men in particular the quality of the meal was the prime consideration. Comments like 'Ah the meal was grand' denoted dissatisfaction. The compliment that every host wanted to hear was 'Jaysus, t'was a mighty feed' – 'mighty' was the ultimate accolade. Anything less was failure. My father glowed contentedly during my wedding day when he heard 'mighty' recurring in a number of conversations throughout the day.

Rural proposals were often unique. For example, every Christmas one of our neighbours would tell the story of the key which had unlocked his heart forever and led to his proposal of marriage. He'd been away and, when he came back to Ireland, he travelled the three miles to give a young lady a Christmas present – because she was now his sweetheart. He arrived to find a tense situation. A full-scale row had broken out between her father and their next-door neighbour on Christmas morning. Both men owned mares, but the mares had foaled in the same field. One foal was stillborn and both mares were licking and nursing the other. His neighbour – the sweetheart – had resolved this tricky predicament by saying, 'Lead the foal into the stream down at the end of the field and the real mother will follow it in.' Her ruse worked and to her father's delight it was his horse which waded into the cold stream without hesitation.

My neighbour knew a wise head when he saw one. This was the

woman for him. Their love was like the Victoria Falls. It went on and on, though never softly.

## The Wedding March

Weddings served an important unifying function in a community, particularly in rural Ireland in the 1960s. In many places, any wedding was to be the wedding of the year. In fact, it was generally the only wedding in the parish that particular year: another silent reminder of the ravages of emigration in rural Ireland. Everybody in the parish was asked, well nearly everyone. The odd person was left at home. The official explanation for her absence could be that she had a suspect heart. The real reason would be that she only gave a Mass card as a present and so would not pay her way at the reception.

In many cases, the men in particular were not exactly in the first flush of youth. Marriage would provide them with a welcome escape from what Patrick Kavanagh evocatively described as 'the purgatory of middle-aged virginity'. For some, what was much more important than any romantic consideration was the fact that the groom was getting a 'good catch'.

The invitations went out a month before the wedding. As invitation cards were a novelty for some people, they were puzzled by what the initials RSVP meant. They were quickly informed that it was a nice way of saying, 'Please spend voraciously on the present.'

By the time my 'big day' arrived I could barely control my nervous excitement within myself. My neighbour was the first to ask the question that was on everybody's lips, 'Will the weather hold?' He scratched his head as he looked up at the sky. 'Be Gawd I think it will,' he said cheerfully. When his wife looked doubtful he revised his opinion as he scrutinised the heavens for a second time. 'Then again it mightn't,' he said anxious to cover all the options.

The congregation were seated in the church minutes before I arrived. The women availed themselves of the opportunity to check who was wearing what. Some of the men looked bored out of their minds but consoled themselves with thoughts of the drink and the chat later on. Advice was doled out with wanton abandon: 'Marriage is like cycling a bicycle for two. When both partners pedal at the same time it is possible to get over the top of the hill, but if only one person is pedalling it is virtually impossible.' And: 'The most important thing is to be able to sacrifice what we are for what we are about to become.'

After the ceremony the photographer went into overdrive, circling the happy couple – Jimmy and me! – like a swarm of bees. The reception saw the usual telegrams being read out – with the customary sprinkling of risqué jokes about weather forecasts and a hot night ahead. The best man acted as an efficient censor, skilfully extricating any really blue or bawdy elements in deference to the presence of the clergy and nuns.

Conversation flowed as freely as the drink. During the meal the focus of the chat in certain quarters were the recent 'merger' of Jimmy and his blushing bride. Then the singing started, or more correctly, the murdering of songs like the 'The Merry Ploughboy'. For myself, my wedding and the build-up to it were the fulfilment of my life's dream.

It was great saving to get married. The anticipation was incredible, but we had a setback because I lost my job. This was not a new experience for me. My friends had a joke that, wherever I went, the factory closed. I had no real skills to move to a different sort of job. I had been doing a typing course at night in the youth club but when I met Jimmy, I lost interest. I was never really academically minded. Although I often went to the library in Athlone, I spent most of my time there looking out over the Shannon. I always tried to carry my Walter Macken books, that way people would think I was very intelligent.

We did the saving, but it was my parents who arranged our huge big wedding for us. Jimmy and I didn't really have anything to do with it, and we didn't know half the people there either! After the reception, when I was out of my dress, one of the guests said to me, 'Wasn't the bride beautiful', not realising that it was me. My aunt Marie had bought me a beautiful white dress with a huge long train and the long veil. I had lost a lot of weight for the wedding, which made me feel very good about myself. It was also great to have my little sister as a flower girl. I can still hear the beautiful singing of '*Ave Maria*' at the wedding ceremony.

We missed the early train for Galway where we would honeymoon. A bed and breakfast was our destination. We were shown to our room by a nun, which I found very embarrassing. In fact, the place seemed full of nuns (they were having some kind of conference!). I had twenty pounds for my honeymoon, but I couldn't wait to get back from my honeymoon to have everyone call me Mrs Carroll.

All the young me ever wanted out of life was to fall in love. When I married my ideal man on that golden summer's day I felt like a character out of a Mills & Boon novel. I had never realised such bliss existed in real life. On the day of my marriage, fantasy and reality joined together. The world was ours. With Jimmy, I had great plans for the future, great hopes and great ambitions.

*Great Expectations*
The mood of optimism of the swinging sixties still beat strongly in the summer of 1972. Ireland was about to take her place in the EEC and move into the fast lane. The possibilities seemed limitless.

The census returns of the previous year had painted an optimistic, even rosy, picture of a nation at last boldly taking its rightful place among the world's elite. New factories and schools were springing up everywhere. The scourge of emigration had not just been halted – it had been reversed as thousands of people returned from England, America and Australia to the Emerald Isle.

It was a time of extraordinary change. A variety of factors came together like converging lines to produce a social, economic and cultural revolution. Ireland had ceased to be a predominantly agricultural country. Industry and commerce had become more important than farming. As a consequence of this, Ireland had become an urban society, with the majority of people living in towns and cities instead of living off the land. Whereas in the 1950s, emigration had haemorrhaged the Irish population to the extent that most of the country's finest and brightest had left the country, by the early 1970s, Ireland had become a country of young people.

For the first time since the Great Famine, the Irish population recorded an increase. The cancer of emigration had abated. And for the first time since the Middle Ages, the vulnerable Irish economy was showing promising signs of being able to support itself.

Other changes were less tangible but no less significant. Educational standards were much higher. The introduction of free secondary education in the late 1960s, by the Minister of Education, Donogh O'Malley, had far-reaching effects. The most obvious manifestation of this was the myriad of yellow school buses, which populated country roads in the early mornings and late afternoons, as they ferried armies of schoolchildren from the country into the towns. However, better education brought new expectations, new ways of thinking and doing and, in many cases, a sharp questioning of what went before.

Ireland had now entered the era of the global village. At the flick of a switch, the world was at the viewer's fingertips. No picture was more dramatic than the sight of Neil Armstrong walking on the moon in July 1969 and uttering the immortal words: 'One small step for man; one giant leap for mankind.'

The sounds of the Beatles were as well known in Longford as they were in London. Although no Irish band could emulate their success at the time, a host of showbands like Larry Cunningham and the Mighty Avons, Eileen Reid and the Cadets, Brendan Bowyer and the Royal Showband, whose famous dance number 'The Hucklebuck' attained extraordinary popularity and became an anthem for a generation of Irish jivers. Radio Luxembourg became more important than Radio Eireann to many young people.


*Every Beginning Is a Promise*

I was quickly to discover that marriage was not to be the bed of roses I had expected.

At that time, no young married couple had their own home. That was the accepted thing. We stayed with my parents for a week. At that stage Jimmy had his passing out ceremony in the army and got his marksman's badge and thus eighteen pounds a week. We then got a flat in MacFarlands in Athlone. We only had two rooms and the kitchen was so tiny it was virtually impossible to do anything.

Adjusting from being a single woman to being a married woman is a very frightening experience. You realise that you are no longer your own person. Although you may love somebody very much, you can feel very trapped. Marriage is totally different to going out with somebody because you have to learn to live with another person and answer to that person and learn their needs.

I'd been going to work for years, but I'd never really had to handle money – I'd not been used to it. I had to have meals ready and look after washing and ironing and think of all the bills, like the ESB. Learning to cope was very difficult because I had to learn everything by myself. It felt like going through a minefield. But the most important lesson we learned was not to let things fester.

The practical tasks gave me a lot of awkward moments and my self-confidence took a battering. Two incidents in particular stand out. Once my mentor Sr Mary Dymphna called when I was serving curry stew to Jimmy. It was pure water because I made it wrong. There was no thickness in it at all. I also remember the first time I had my parents for tea. I'd made my first apple tart. I asked them what they thought of it. They said it was nice enough but it could have done with a bit more sugar.

Still, Jimmy gave me confidence in myself. I didn't realise then that I was attractive – I never wore slacks until Jimmy bought them for me. I always asked the Lord in prayer to leave both of us until we were eighty years of age and that we would die together. I was always afraid Jimmy would die before me and that I wouldn't be able to handle it.

Because of his work in the army, Jimmy was away from home a lot. When he was up in Gormanstown training with the army, his parents came to stay with me. It probably seemed like a good idea to them but I had no privacy.

Then, like many people in the defence forces, Jimmy volunteered for the UN peacekeeping service abroad. He was to go to Cyprus for six months.

I know that he thought it was the right thing for him to do, even though it was going to be tough for me. While I know that army people really learn a lot from that experience, it was a terribly lonely time for me. I was pregnant with my first child, Anthony, at the time.

Many soldiers experience a sense of loneliness when they are away from home for long periods. Jimmy and I wrote to each other every single day; there was not one day while he was in Cyprus that he missed a letter. It's hard enough being away from your husband on your first anniversary, but particularly when you are expecting your first child. And so, I will never forget when he had Treasa Davidson play a request for me for our first anniversary on the radio on *Overseas Requests*.

I have huge admiration for the Defence Forces. The human cost of the Irish UN peacekeeping mission must not be forgotten. Memories of previous tragedies must be preserved. Such as those relatives of the three Irish soldiers killed in the Lebanon in October 1982 as they manned an observation post. One of the soldiers' widows was expecting a baby who her husband would never see.

Peacekeeping has become an integral part of Ireland's heritage. It has given us some of the most significant episodes in the last two generations, such as the mission to the Congo in 1960, which captivated the Irish public, attracting enormous media attention at the time. This interest intensified with the tragic death of Irish soldiers in the course of their duty. Martyrs for the cause of peace, their return from duty touched a deep chord in the psyche of the Irish people. Few events in the last seventy years have precipitated such a groundswell of sympathy. Eighty-five Irish soldiers in the last sixty years have made the ultimate sacrifice with their lives in the cause of Ireland's peacekeeping missions abroad. Experience in locations such as Angola, Cambodia, Central America, Iran and Iraq, Kuwait, Afghanistan and Chad has enabled Ireland to become world leaders in peacekeeping activities.

In the Middle Ages, when Ireland was 'the island of Saints and

Scholars', it was our missionaries who defined the Irish experience abroad. Increasingly today, it is the Irish peacekeepers who encapsulate the best of Ireland's contribution to the world.

It was a real education for me, hearing about the work of these peacekeepers. In Jimmy's case, a feature of the area once they got to Cyprus – or the Lebanon as did many of his colleagues – was that the landscape was despoiled by war debris. An intrinsic part of their observation requirement was the patrolling of the demarcated area, which was a dangerous activity because of the prevalence of landmines.

To a casual observer, there was a relaxed atmosphere and little danger of hostilities breaking out. But beneath the calm exterior a deep distrust remained which led to sporadic bouts of tension. In such a volatile atmosphere, the smallest incident could spark a major crisis, even all-out war. For example, some shepherds might move too close to the fence. This would be interpreted as an attempt to test the army's defences and warning shots would be fired to keep the shepherds away. Jimmy told me how, on one occasion, shots resulted in the death of a shepherd in a situation close to an Irish soldier.

Another day, Jimmy's friend remembers carrying out a fortnightly inspection of the military forces when he saw somebody scrambling for cover. The radar screens picked up incoming aircraft and, sure enough, almost immediately a MiG fighter came very close to the Israeli side of the ceasefire line and then turned away. This was an attempt to test the Israelis and to see what the Israeli response might be. After that, there was an all-out alert by the Israeli soldiers. Had these aircraft crossed over even one centimetre of their borderline, all hell would have broken loose.

One of the first things that grabbed Jimmy's attention was the sight of two armies being deployed against one another. You can always imagine what it must be like, but you really have to experience it for yourself to understand. The tragedy that war brings was something soldiers learned at first hand, particularly the cruel division of families in Cyprus, which meant that they could only communicate with each other through a megaphone.

There were times when things got very tense. Jimmy and his men had a situation where they could not move on a road because there were many landmines stopping them from doing their job. One soldier lost his leg below the knee after a landmine exploded while a unit was in the process of making a roadway safe for use. Five more Irish personnel were injured in the incident, though not as seriously.

The Irish army has a rich tradition of peacekeeping. We had a continuous battalion in the Lebanon for twenty-two years. Their role is to monitor, support and assist: and it is a role we are very familiar with. I had heard all the stories of these great places and it was wonderful for Jimmy to become part of that history.

The Irish are part of a larger multinational United Nations force. The conflicts they are involved in go back a long time. There can be thirty-seven nations involved in the peacekeeping project. From an Irish point of view, the locals always seem delighted to have us because of the way we can get on with people – one of the reasons, surely, why we are such good peacekeepers.

It is an eye-opener to see the legacy of conflict. It's a life experience. It is tough emotionally on the soldiers. It was a terrible shock to them all when there is a horrific tragedy that leaves grieving families in its wake. Many people will know Paul Brady's marvellous song 'The Island' in which he talks about the conflict in Lebanon. He sings about the women and children dying in the street. At its worst, this was a horrific conflict.

The army's main priority is to take practical steps to sustain and improve morale. Their priority is to keep both soldiers and family happy. For example, they ensure that soldiers get mail quickly. It's a trying time for everybody when mail goes astray. A week goes by and regular letter or letters from home fail to arrive. People on the ground and those at home can get very lonely. You have to remember that there were no mobile phones when Jimmy went to Cyprus for six months, let alone emails or social media.

For individual soldiers events like anniversaries, birthdays and first Holy Communions can be particularly tough. Worst of all is Christmas. People become very conscious of missing their families at that time. The army makes every possible effort to recreate the type of Christmas atmosphere soldiers would experience at home, but this can be very difficult, especially in a different climate. Even so, the army pulls out all the stops with a fabulous Christmas dinner and a lovely midnight service so there are echoes of home – but it is still a poor substitute for Christmas with families. Depression was a constant threat especially when people got bad news like a relation-ship break-up. You had to be very attentive for signs of death by suicide in extreme cases.

These are the problems anybody who is away for a long time has to cope with. To make the adjustment back to your family can be difficult.

## Home Alone

While Jimmy was away I was longing for his return every day. It was a very long six months. But there was the odd moment of joy.

I can still remember the first time Anthony kicked. I was very apprehensive about going into the maternity hospital. Things were very tight money wise for Jimmy and me, so they only clothes I had were hand-me-downs. I had no maternity coat and only one of my mother's maternity dresses. I had a horrible old dressing gown and I was terrified at the prospects of having to pay for the medical expenses.

The first time I felt my baby in my arms it was as if the Lord was giving me a lift. Little did I know, though, what he had in store for me. Anthony was born on the 21st of July 1973, when Jimmy was in Cyprus; he was three months old before his father saw him for the first time.

## A Test to Come

Shakespeare was as prolific in his insights as in his words:

> 'Love's not Time's fool, though rosy lips and cheeks
> Within his bending sickle's compass come;
> Love alters not with his brief hours and weeks,
> But bears it out even to the edge of doom.'
> — 'Sonnet 116'

I was to learn the wisdom of this insight all too painfully.

# 6

# The Morning After Optimism

*'There exists only the present instant . . . a Now which always and without end is itself new. There is no yesterday nor any tomorrow, but only Now, as it was a thousand years ago and as it will be a thousand years hence.'*

— MEISTER ECKHART

The deep silence of the Irish countryside swallowed up the music of change hungrily. There would not be a more exciting time to get married and to plan a new life. It was a time to dream and every dream seemed achievable.

For the new Mr and Mrs Carroll, things could not have looked better in December 1972 when we discovered that we would be first-time parents the following year. It was an early Christmas present.

For me the only slightly disconcerting feature of my early months as a married woman was that I began to fall from time to time around the house. I put it down simply to a poor choice of footwear. As I am only five feet two inches I convinced myself it was because I was wearing high-heeled shoes. Whenever I toppled over I blamed it entirely on my shoes. It never even crossed my mind that it might be a sign that all was not well inside me.

My pregnancy was a difficult one, but I knew that many women had problematic pregnancies without incurring any long-term damage. I assumed that once I had my baby I would return to normal. Anyway a little – or even a lot – of pain and distress was small price to pay for realising my life's dream of becoming a mother.

This opinion was confirmed when Anthony, a healthy baby boy, was born. Euphoria is too mild a term to describe the elation and exhilaration I felt; I was scarcely able to contain my joy. No words can adequately convey my feelings. It was not just parental pride. It was a sense of belonging to a new family unit, of being part of something special.

There are moments when it seems the gods are on your side – when nothing can possibly go wrong. A lifetime seemed to be crowded into the space of a second. Although I had been under constant pressure before Anthony was born, it seemed that the tide had turned in my favour again.

Thoughts of being the perfect mother were uppermost in my mind when I made the short journey home from hospital. It was a journey into the unknown. The life of the first-time mother is a curious and fascinating mixture of happiness and stress. The pleasure of the little coy smiles, the sheer bliss of holding the baby in my arms, the excitement of showing off the baby to relatives and friends is balanced by worrying about ensuring that the baby is neither too hot nor too cold, sleepless nights with crying and feedings, dirty nappies and, most alarmingly, the fear of the frail new creature getting ill.

In the period of adjustment after childbirth, I had only a faint suspicion that my tiredness, stress and physical discomfort were anything out of the ordinary. I listened more attentively to any radio discussions on the subject of post-natal depression. Perhaps my condition was not unusual. Any time the pain became too much, I needed only to see Anthony's smiling face to think that I would have suffered a hundred times more to feel part of the miracle of life.

Like every mother, I felt that my child was very special. That feeling sustained me whenever my discomfort became overwhelming.

Like a bolt out of the blue, I was to find that my dreams of domestic bliss lay on shaky foundations. I shiver at the memory of the event that sparked off my descent into despair.

Anthony was ten months old. It was my parents' wedding anniversary. Jimmy and I went out with them on a Saturday night to celebrate. I've always loved dancing since I was a child – and so, I danced the whole night. The next morning when I woke up my leg felt funny. I put it down to doing too much dancing the night before. As the day wore on my leg gave me increasing pain. I promised never to dance again.

The following morning Jimmy suggested that I should go and see our doctor. My leg was still feeling funny, as if I had pins and needles in it all the time, and a tired nagging pain in it as well. I made the effort to go to my doctor, but found it was too much for me. When Jimmy came home he rang the doctor, but he was unavailable. The doctor on call promised to come out and see me. His prognosis was that I had been struck down by the flu that was going around.

That night I lay awake all night. My pain was rapidly becoming intolerable. I knew in my heart and soul that my problem was more serious than the flu. My own doctor called to see me the following morning. I confided to him that a few weeks previously I had fallen against Anthony's cot while opening the bedroom curtains. The doctor suspected that my medical difficulties emanated from that incident and speculated that the root cause of my problem was a slipped disc. He suggested that I might make the journey to Tipperary to visit a Mr Heffernan, who was reputed to be able to cure a slipped disc.

This was to be the start of a long and tense odyssey for both myself and Jimmy, to establish the reason for my illness. It was a rollercoaster of different opinions, contradictory analyses and frustration.

There were many cul-de-sacs before the correct diagnosis was arrived at. Although the final outcome would be terrifying, it was a merciful relief to be freed from the fog of uncertainty that enveloped me.


*A Horror Story*

I recorded those years of my life in a journal. As I look back on it, my diary makes for harrowing reading. Pain screams off every page. What is most striking about the document is that, although my physical pain and distress were enormous, the really deep wounds were caused by the attitudes of other people to me.

Reading the journal I can hear two voices: one which is deeply appreciative of the love, care and understanding shown to me by my family, friends and health-care professionals; the other has been hurt by the attitudes of a minority of people to me during my long illness.

Although my own personality did not change, the attitude of some people towards me did in a very obvious and disturbing way. I was shocked by the change – the transformation was incredible. I did not want to be mollycoddled or fussed over, but I hoped for a bit of sympathy and sensitivity. Instead, some people who did not understand my illness thought I was feigning injury just to avoid working or taking responsibility. My former friends and relatives – even some close relatives, who shared this opinion – did not mince their words. The words cut through me like a knife. In describing those comments in my diary, I look back now and find that my tone is one of wounded offence. Despite the passing of the years I have never been able to erase that memory.

One of the clearest lessons to emerge from the journal is that to care for somebody is radically different from pity. Care is constructive, pity is destructive. Like a rock on the ocean being battered by the crashing waves, the victim of pity is slowly and torturously eroded in piecemeal fashion – each little attack seeps away another little fragment of personal dignity.

There are also very mixed feelings about the health-care profession in the journal. On the one hand, there is great gratitude and admiration for the nurses in particular and also some kind doctors who were able not only to give me treatment but also to nurture my self-image and feeling of well-being. Those caring medical staff helped me to see the healing hands of Jesus in human form; they were people who had the empathy and understanding that my perilous emotional condition craved for. They saw how it was necessary not just to cater for my physiological needs, but also for my emotional and psychological needs as well. Despite my physical disabilities, they helped me fulfil my potential as a human person.

We often use words very casually. What do we really mean when we speak of love, truth or beauty? In our time, the concepts of 'care' and the 'caring professions' have become almost clichéd. Patients with mysterious illnesses, by virtue of their increased vulnerability, must entrust a greater part of themselves to the goodwill of their doctors. They hope, justifiably, for a response to that trust which treats them with human concern and respect, as well as with professional knowledge and skill. As a norm, they are not disappointed in that hope.

In some cases I would be.

There are wounds from those encounters that will never heal.


### High Hopes
All patients go to hospitals and doctors' surgeries with apprehensions and their own particular expectations. When these patients are treated as human beings, and not just as bed numbers, their fears are

allayed and their expectations are met with excellent care, empathetic treatment, and with continuing good health.

However, the practical problems facing doctors on a daily basis, such as the need to fit emergency treatments into crowded schedules, stress and administrative problems limit the doctor's ability to reach and maintain the high standard which the medical profession is famous for. On a number of occasions I was to receive hurried explanations wrapped in technical jargon and language I was unable to understand from doctors who did not seem to possess the ability to share in my pain and anguish.

Care is not simply a feeling of benevolence to the patient, but above all a way of relating. I felt that my disease – whatever it was, none of them seemed to know exactly – was all that mattered to some of the doctors who treated me, rather than me, the person who was suffering from illness. A striking feature of my journal is the belief that the role of 'carer' requires a fundamental respect for the other if the relationship is to be constructive. Care ought not be given in an imperialistic way, in a way which deprives the patient of her or his human dignity.

There is a strong undercurrent of anger in this section of my life because I clearly believe my own dealings with doctors undermined my dignity. As a result, for a crucial part of my life, when I could fairly have described myself as a 'physical wreck', I lost all faith in doctors.

## The Cloud of Unknowing

'It's a long way to Tipperary', according to the song, but as Jimmy drove down to the 'home of hurling' it seemed a very short distance to travel if it offered an end to my pain. Hopes of an early resolution to my discomfort were dashed when Mr Heffernan informed me that the problem was not a slipped disc, but something much more serious. After another consultation a few days later with my doctor I was referred to Navan hospital for tests. I wince as I recall the next chapter of my medical voyage of discovery.

In Navan hospital I was put on leg traction for a few weeks. When I was sent home it seemed the treatment had done the trick, but within a fortnight or so my leg started to act up again. This time, when I was brought back to Navan, it was discovered that I was allergic to the leg strapping. They put me on a pelvis strap. I found it hurt me. Shortly after, my pelvis was X-rayed.

One day a doctor got four nurses to hold my legs and two to hold my arms while he injected me in the pelvis. As you can imagine, I found this very distressing. After that experience I was told that for similar infections I would receive an anaesthetic, which would put me to sleep. Within a few days I was informed that there was really nothing wrong with me and I was sent home with a pair of crutches. I was assured that the crutches would give me the support I needed, but unfortunately it was not to be.

The relief at being home again was quickly dissipated as I found out that even with the crutches I was unable to maintain my balance consistently. As my condition deteriorated, I heard glowing reports about a specialist in Jervis Street hospital. I requested a referral from my doctor. He was happy to do so, but first he wanted me to see a psychiatrist. I stared at him, my fragile world facing slow disintegration, all feeling crystallising into that one frightening word which he had just uttered with apparent ease. My mind struggled with this alien concept, but it could not absorb this bombshell. All kinds of hideous images entered my head – of shadowy figures in white coats and with menacing eyes locking me in a cell. My world would never be normal again, or so it seemed to me at the time.

Drawing on the last spark of vitality that was left in my by now punch-drunk brain I heard my own voice clumsily asking, 'Will I be all right? Am I psychiatrically unwell? Will I have to go home?' My doctor's reply was warm and understanding, but he did not in any way assuage my fears. I went home in a trance, oblivious to Jimmy's best efforts to console me. I shudder as I recall that stage of my illness.

I went to see the psychiatrist in Athlone. I was more afraid of who would see me there than what the doctor would say. I was petrified that people who would know me would think I was mentally unwell and that I would have to be put in a 'mental hospital'.

The doctor asked me a lot of questions and I answered them all. After I was with him I was let off to Jervis Street, as I wanted. I was too confused to put two and two together to see that if I did in fact have a mental illness I would not have been sent to Dublin, but to the dreaded 'mental home', or at the very least I would have been put on drugs for those with mental troubles.

Right through that period of 1972 to 1978, I was constantly terrified that someone would send me to a mental hospital and that the doctors would change their minds and say I was insane. I have talked to many other MS sufferers since and they all had the same fear. When I started to lose my physical power, I felt it was good to have a sign that I wasn't mentally unwell. It sounds funny but I think that is the way with a lot of people with MS when there is a sign that it's not a mental illness, they feel happier. So many people out there have MS and they are suffering from tiredness and very mild other symptoms that people cannot recognise, unless they have MS themselves.

People don't understand MS. Some people think that the MS sufferers are trying to dodge work or get out of things or are neurotic. You can't imagine what it must be like for those people, in the workplace or at home. I don't blame the families – the problem is the education to explain MS is inadequate. Thankfully that situation is being rectified now. It's long overdue. Please God it will help to change attitudes to MS.

## Jekyll and Hyde

The trip to Jervis Street did not bring the long-hoped-for cure. I was informed that I was suffering from back strain and given tablets. Over the next few months, I started to fall more frequently and drop things from my right hand.

It was at this time that I started to live two lives, one when I was on my own – my real self – and the other when Jimmy came home or when there was anybody else in the house other than little Anthony, who was blissfully oblivious to my physical condition, when I tried to conceal any signs of illness from public display. I knew something awful was happening but I couldn't trust myself to talk about it. Maybe if I swept it under the carpet it would go away. It wasn't really the pain that I was afraid of, but a deeper anxiety about the stigma of 'madness'.

I kept saying to myself, 'Whatever news you're given today, you're going to get through it, you've got to be positive, you have no choice.' Tears began to flow down my cheeks; I was on my own on this one, and it was tough. I never let on to anyone that the doctor had wanted to see me urgently. I was going to take this on the chin no matter what news was to await me when I got into that doctor's surgery. All sorts of thoughts ran through my head, 'What is wrong with me? Is there anything else that can happen to me that can push me over the edge altogether?' One really bad day I remember looking up to the ceiling and closing my eyes while saying, 'Lord, into your hands I commend my spirit.'

There were many times when I was forced to stay in bed because I was unable to walk. On those occasions I explained to Jimmy that I had pulled or strained a muscle in my back. My situation would get much worse before it got better.

Through the next few years I had trouble on and off. I would not be too good and then I would be all right for a while. I remember going to my doctor because I was so tired. He took some blood tests and sent them away to see if there was any reason for the tiredness. When they came back he told me not to be burning the candle at both ends and to stay in more at night and rest. Little did he know that we could not afford to go out. Not only had we not had the money to go out for a long time, but also we could not afford our dinner the last few days before pay day.

The problems I had were not just with doctors. People can be very cruel. Unless you are in a wheelchair, on crutches, or walking with a stick, they don't believe you are sick. I used to hear people saying, 'Don't be stupid' and 'You are suffering from your nerves' when I needed support badly.

I shied away from people. It was a horrific point in my life. I find it very painful to re-read my journal from that time because all that hurt is in it.

Thanks be to God I'm over that myself, but I know others are going through it today, and not just MS sufferers. People don't realise you can be sick in many ways. It doesn't have to be physical, it doesn't have to show itself to others, and the worst thing of all is people who have worries, because if you have physical pains you can go to the doctor and get a tablet, but if you have worries, financial or personal, you may not have anyone to talk to and have to sort them out alone. They are the people I really feel for.

We moved to Cloghan, Co Offaly, in 1976. I was pregnant with our daughter Cora at the time. Like my pregnancy with Anthony, it was a very difficult one. Because of a series of infections I spent most of the time in Portiuncula hospital in Ballinasloe.

Cora was born on the 14th of December 1976. When Jimmy visited the proud mother for the first time in hospital, the feeling of being locked in an embrace with my husband would linger in my mind for ever. However, that was when things got worse – much worse.

### The Hand that Rocks the Cradle

When I returned home I cherished the belief that my horror story would end. I felt that I had served my sentence and, in the difficult hours, I consoled myself with the thoughts that at least things couldn't get worse.

I was wrong.

My problems were like an onion. There were layers and layers of interlocking ones, feeding off each other. I could not trust myself to walk or to hold anybody or anything in my hand. At the back of my consciousness was the fear that I was losing my mind and never out of my thoughts was the nightmarish spectacle of some official from an unknown body talking my two precious children away from me and declaring me to be an unfit mother.

I was scared. I kept saying to myself, 'Whatever news you're given today, you're going to get through it, you got to be positive, you have no choice.'

I was scared telling my husband that I was unable to look after my children. I had to take hold of this situation and turn my approach into a proactive one.

I had no choice: it was my journey and mine alone.

I had to find the strength to go on. That was my way forward, keeping a good positive thought on things, even when the rug was firmly being taken from under my feet.

There were times, though, when I cried my eyes out. I was confused, angry and stunned. *What is wrong with me?* I screamed silently. *Is there anything else that can happen to me that can push me over the edge altogether?* I could feel a sense of, Where is God in all of this? Is He behind it all and if He is, I wished He could make things better.

But things were getting no better.

I feared that things would get worse before they got better.

I was right.

What I had not bargained for, though, was that things would get worse before they would get even worse.

Much, much worse.

It is not until now that I can stand back and reflect over the last few years and understand what has happened and really tune into what life is about and why we are all here on earth. It is through the gift of life that we can understand the meaning of love and relationships between all people; through our own suffering we are comforted and through our comfort we learn to love everybody.

At the time, though, I constantly feared that I would be whisked away by some bureaucrat to a psychiatric institution. Since my husband was a sergeant in the army, much of his time was spent on border duty and, despite his best efforts to spend every possible minute at home, I was left on my own a lot. We lived in a mobile home, near Jimmy's parents' house. With no running water, it was not the ideal environment for a sick mother with a baby and a young child. But hopes of an easier home were on hold, as my illness put a huge strain on the family's finances. Frequent extended stays in hospital and visits to doctors and specialists as well as expensive medication put an impossible burden on Jimmy's salary. Yet the greatest tragedy was that I could not be the type of mother I wanted to be.

## A Mother Without Mothering

Even now my eyes moisten as I think about those days. I do not simply remember it, I re-live it. I replay each incident in my mind. I still remember how Jimmy's face would betray all the emotions of the era itself. His hands gesticulating and his voice animated with passion and pain.

It was a very difficult time for me because the only way I could hold my children, when they were babies, was to hold them in a double bed and make walls of pillows around me in case I dropped them. I could never actually go to a cot or a pram and pick up my baby. I found that very, very hard. I also began to have periods of black-outs after Cora was born. I never told Jimmy anything about this, or the fact that I could only cuddle Cora when she was sitting well back in the bed so that if my right arm got tired or numb I could put her down gently.

I often found when I went out to collect water I would wake up on the ground and the bucket of water spilled all over me. The same thing used to happen to me inside the mobile home.

Our little boy Anthony had not yet started school, so I used to tell him that we were playing Cowboys and Indians and, when I was hit by the Indians, I would play dead. He was to make sure that Cora was on her side and to put a blanket at her stomach and back. He was to pretend that his daddy and the army were coming to rescue us. All I could do was hope that I wasn't out cold for too long.

At this stage I was constantly tired. I was also getting bad head-aches. I could not see very well and found it very hard to wash or iron clothes.

I had to have both my children by caesarean section. I thought the reason I was suffering so much was that I didn't have them in the normal way.

Looking back now, there are things I can never get back, like holding my babies, and not being too tired to hold them, and being like other mothers. That was the saddest part of it. I tried as best I could but I missed out on a lot. That's the great tragedy of my life. My hope at that time was that someday in the future Cora and Anthony would get married and I would be blessed with grandchil-dren. Then I could make up for lost time.

My blood runs cold as I remember the might-have-beens. Much of my time was spent in a trance. I have a mental blank about some of the weeks and months. Fear ran through me in the form of panic attacks when I lost my senses like a foretaste of hell. Much later on, I would discover that the cause of all this was epilepsy.

Things came to a head in September 1977 when Anthony started school. By this time we had sold our mobile home and we were waiting to move into a council house until we could afford to build one of our own. While we waited for our new home, we had moved in with Jimmy's parents.

Gradually the pain in my head became unbearable and my vision became very poor. On Wednesday 14th September my father-in-law, who worked as a bus driver, had a brain haemorrhage. That day was one of my worst with my headache. I remember that Jimmy was patting cold cloths on my head that night when his mother came in crying to tell him that his father was dead.

She then told us that he was brought to Athlone hospital. My brother-in-law stayed with her and we went down to see what had happened. When Jimmy and I went down to the hospital, his father was not dead but in a coma. I still was not feeling too good but did not want to worry Jimmy any further. He had more than enough on his plate as it was.

Two days later, Jimmy's father died. Naturally this was very tough on Jimmy, but it was also very tough on me because Joe was one of the very few people who was always kind to me when other people were telling me I was stupid. I didn't actually look sick, so perhaps I can't blame them.

Before going to Joe's funeral, I went to the doctor for an injection for the pain. He was anxious that I should go to hospital but I told him that was not possible because Jimmy needed me at the time. My most vivid memory of my father-in-law's funeral is of two total strangers helping me off the ground at the graveside.

After the funeral, my mother-in-law took a slight heart attack and was sent immediately to Tullamore hospital. The next day I went with Jimmy and his aunt to see her. I still had a headache and all of a sudden everything became blurred and I could only see colours all joined together. Although we were talking to my mother-in-law at her bedside I felt that she was very far away from me and that she was whispering. I went out to the corridor, thinking the odd sensations would go away. The next thing I remember I was lying on a different surface. They had put me on a bed. I had obviously collapsed. I could only see shadows but Jimmy seemed to be there. My parents came to see me later, but I remember very little about that time in hospital.

I discovered later that I had been in intensive care. After a few days, when my sight started to come back and my hearing was all right, I was brought back to an ordinary ward. Jimmy told me that he had asked the doctor over and over again to send me to Dublin to see a specialist. The doctor in charge told him that he was bringing a doctor, who was a psychiatrist, to see me from Port Laoise. He asked me a lot of questions and when I had finished answering I asked him if my problems were caused by my nerves. I explained that because my husband was in the army and away from home a lot I had to be both a mother and a father to my children. If it was my nerves I wanted to know what I could do to step out of it and pull myself together to end my nightmare. He told me that I did not need his services but suggested to my doctor that I should have a brain scan in Dublin.

Although the scan was arranged, a doctor told me in the most emphatic terms that no matter what anyone else said he believed the problem was with my nerves.

On Friday the 29th of September, after what seemed like an eternity to me, I was let out of hospital. I was on no medication except painkillers. I felt that doctors did not understand me or didn't seem to really want to help. I made a vow to never tell a doctor if anything strange happened to me. I decided that a kidney infection was the only thing I would visit a doctor for.

My rock-like faith and my devotion to my family drove my ability to endure the apparently unendurable. It was very difficult at the time, but we had something special in our home, we had Jesus and Mary, and then we had a wonderful marriage. Jimmy and I were one another's best friend as well as husband and wife. There's not two people, we are as one. When we got married, some people said we were too young to know what we were doing. However, our love is very special and it was only through our difficulties that we found out how special our love was. There was always that special quality – giving. Even when the children came along they realised that all we had was one another. They all gave. It was never just take.

Jimmy used to come home in the evening and try to be cheerful and, even though I was in pain, I would try and do the same because I knew it was hard on him. I was very lucky. We always felt that in spite of everything we were very lucky as a family. We always had the Rosary and that brought us many miracles.

Looking back, it is difficult to find any moments of Jimmy making any concession to despair even when pain was the background music to my life so long, nor of doubting the power of God in my life. My faith was not simply a consolation. It animates my every waking moment. Sometimes my faith appears almost childlike.

When little Anthony started school at least some of the pressure was taken off me as a mother, but my constant fear was that I would do something which would accidentally inflict pain on Cora or, worse still, cause her irreparable harm.

Every day this fear increased as I sank to each new level of degradation. One Sunday evening, during Mass, I collapsed in the church. When I came around and tried to gather my scattered wits, I did not know where I was.

This marked the beginning of the second, and even more horrendous, phase of my nightmare.

# 7

# Hard Times

*'Come, take heart, find healing,*
*live again, love again,*
*maybe even more than you did before.'*

— J.J. YOUNG, *Worldwide Wound Healing*

Eventually, that day in the church, through my drunken-like stupor my senses returned and I recognised my neighbour, Lily Daly. The realisation hit me with brutal suddenness that I could not depend on my body and mind for long. The die was cast.

My memories of the time between 1977 and 1978 are blurred. Blackouts became as normal a pattern in my life as showers in April. But it was to be my other recurring complaint, kidney infections, that would send me back to hospital – this time to St Vincent's at Elm Park in Dublin. Jimmy's army duties necessitated an extended stay in Cork. He could not constantly be taking time off to look after his sick wife. It was to be our ultimate nightmare – both our children would experience great disruption as a consequence.

## The Crowning with Thorns

Even though I knew there was no alternative, I despised myself for it. I had dreamed so long of being the perfect mother but now I felt a total failure. Although much of my fears and deep-seated anxieties for myself and my children were totally irrational, I felt overwhelmed. The physical separation from my children was symbolic – a sign that my life and dreams were disintegrating totally.

In a curious sense the most effective treatment for me in hospital came from the patients not from the doctors. My self-pity, if not entirely vanished, was greatly diminished because I could see that my own pain was neither extraordinary nor unbearable. That discovery brought me a morsel of comfort. A week of seemingly endless tests failed to furnish any clues about my condition. I felt the chill winds of total panic when I was told that I was to be examined by the neurologist.

I was sitting up in bed when he came into the ward, he introduced himself and told me that he was a nerve specialist. I think he saw the look on my face because he pointed to his head and said, 'Not there, but nerves of the body.' He asked me a lot of questions but I did not understand what was happening to me. I was still so afraid that if I told him he would put me into a mental hospital. I really wanted just to go home and hide from the doctors.

After a few days, the neurologist asked when my husband would be up. I explained that Jimmy was on an important army exercise in Cork. I think the hospital got in touch with the barracks in Athlone and they got Jimmy to a phone in Cork. The next thing I knew Jimmy was at my bedside. Even my twisted mind was aware that it was a most unusual time for visitors.

The specialist wanted to see Jimmy alone. I knew he was very worried when he returned. I asked him what was wrong, but he said there was nothing. We chatted for a while and suddenly he asked me for a biro. He wrote something on his hand, trying to hide his hand as he wrote. When I asked him what he wanted to write he said it was something he had to remember for the army. I knew instinctively he was hiding something from me – after all, I know Jimmy so well I can almost read his mind – so I grabbed his hand and there I saw two words.

MULTIPLE SCLEROSIS.

I made him tell me truth about my illness. He answered that the doctor had told him not to worry me by telling me anything and that the reason he wrote it on his hand was because it was a mouthful to remember. When I asked him to tell me if it was MS or not he said it was, and then: had I ever heard of it? I told him I'd read it about a week earlier in a magazine and I thought it was a slow paralysis. The doctor had told him it could remain mild or I could end up in a wheelchair or bed for life. Only time would tell. He also said I was lucky I hadn't been put in a mental hospital years earlier.

When I left hospital I did not have much time to think about my condition. My grandmother was in Mullingar hospital and, on our way home from Dublin, we called in to see her. She died within fifteen minutes of us arriving. It was a week before I noticed that people were treating me as if I, too, was dying.

I did not know the meaning of MS. I thought it was something that was going to get better and go away. When I went back to hospital for a check-up, I was put on a course of tablets. I was forced to get 'home help' because I really could not manage on my own. Things got so bad that I could not dress myself or even drink a cup of tea without spilling it. Above all, I was always tired.

I have no doubt that I would have given up earlier only for Jimmy. However, one day, later on, he brought me a cup of coffee in the sitting room. Instead of putting it in my hand he left it on the table beside me. I asked him to pass it to me but he refused, saying he was not going to rush around me all the time. At that stage I was boiling with anger. I was mad with him and suspected that he did not want me anymore. There and then I resolved that no illness was going to get the better of me as long as I could fight it. From then on, if it took me all day to dress so be it. A few years afterwards, I asked Jimmy about the incident with the coffee and the table. He told me that he knew that if I got mad nothing could keep me down – and it worked. My illness, no matter how bad I got, came last in my life; my husband and my children came first.

## God Makes the Back for the Burden

My good resolutions were tested many times. Until my diagnosis in 1978, because he was constantly hearing from a number of different doctors and specialists that there was nothing wrong with his wife, Jimmy began to suspect that I was overreacting. And before my MS diagnosis, all the best medical opinion was that there was essentially nothing wrong with me apart from kidney infections. It was not what was said, but what was implied. In the long term, the best course of action for Jimmy was not to mollycoddle me – 'You have to be cruel to be kind.' I was devastated. On top of my physical problems, it seemed that my husband had lost his love for me.

It nearly wrecked my marriage. I felt wretched and alone. It was the worst time of my life because I had no support or understanding when I needed it. Because I was supposed to be overreacting, Jimmy seemed not to want to know so I stopped telling him if things went wrong and if my body was not working the way it should. One time on a visit to the hospital, a doctor had even asked me if I was going to keep wasting his time and had made me look childish and stupid. So, in a way, Jimmy's attitude was understandable.

## *Prejudice and Loss of Pride*

Worse still was the guilt which intruded into my muddled mind whenever I thought of what I could not do for my children. My frail mental state reeled from the repeated blows of what I didn't do for them. It took years for me to be released from that prison without walls. My soul strove to survive within a vortex of competing voices swirling around like a raging storm. Dreams were essential for my emotional survival, elevating my mind above the junk hoarded there. Dreams were a theatre of boundless possibilities and lofty visions, disturbing what was and inventing what was not. Past, present and future became one. Determination, derision, dejection and delirium were interspersed.

Of course I could not but think of the problems I was causing for my husband. The sunshine had left my life. Laughter was but a fading memory. Tears were an inadequate vehicle for my grief. I sometimes felt that I had lost a large part of my own self. My tower of strength had crumbled, burned and been reduced to ashes. My whole life was precariously perched on my wounded family. Emotionally I could only snatch at the crumbs from other people's dustbins. Laden down with the weights and financial pressures of this world, it was difficult to radiate anything but grimness. Yet by some miracle – more accurately through calm resilience and irrepressible spirit – I offered my family a love that defied limitation as best I could.

For all my problems I was still under the spell of that timeless and universal hunger of all human beings for happiness. But, as I stumbled along this universal procession, even more obstacles blighted the landscape.

And to add to my sorrows, the well of sympathy from relatives had run dry.

The first indication I had of things to come arrived in the shape of a cousin. With her customary lack of tact her opening words to Jimmy were: 'Marion is just pretending to be sick because she is lazy.' This authoritative assertion was not open to contradiction. The last word chilled Jimmy to the bone. It was an accusation, an indictment of us all. The inflection in her voice more than the words themselves suggested that Jimmy had some culpability in the situation. Her insensitive comments were almost as devasting as the news of my illness.

He was too dumfounded to respond. 'Lazy' was bad enough but 'pretending' was totally incapacitating. And still the cousin's incessant monologue went on. Whoever said silence is golden knew what they were talking about. Jimmy tried to shut his ears. It was the only paltry defence mechanism he could muster. He would have needed cotton wool to drown her incoherent rambling. Each new sentence launched a fresh incision in his frail emotional condition. She then embarked on a litany of case histories of people with any kind of illness she ever knew about or dreamed about. From time to time she drew analogies with my condition. Each unfavourable comparison cut like a knife.

## Circles of Support

On the other hand, while I was detained in hospital for weeks a small if steady stream of neighbours and relatives called to enquire about my welfare. In adversity we found out who our friends really were. It was evident in the difference between the concerned and the simply curious.

Increasingly our house took on the hallmarks of a home for the bedraggled and bewildered. We were inundated with advice. A variety of experts were quoted. The classic was a comment: 'A fella in a pub said she will be normal in six months if ye feed her goat's milk.'

The wisdom of distant cousins, mothers-in-law and casual acquaintances was cited with the same authority as the World Health Organisation. People with not an ounce of medical competence pontificated with absolute certainty, even omniscience. Much totally absurd advice was offered to Jimmy. 'Make sure to give her plenty of oranges. That will make her better.'

These do-gooders had honourable intentions, but the pious platitudes were an insult to my husband's intelligence.

Such was my descent into depression that I confided my anxieties to a close relative. It was a major lapse of judgement. I could not have picked a more unsympathetic shoulder to cry on. The woman launched into a tirade on the evils of a nanny state with her characteristically caustic tongue. 'Those friggin spongers should get up off their arses and onto their bikes.'

The phrase 'the nanny state' was a new one to me. Although I had very little economic or political knowledge, I found the very language my relative was using callous in the extreme. I was all for a nanny state if it prevented young mothers having to cry themselves to sleep every night wondering about where the money for next week's food would come from, or how they would finance purchasing shoes and clothing for their children in the winter. A state which fostered laziness, idleness or slavish dependence was clearly not a consummation to be devoutly wished for. Neither were the living conditions of a married childless couple in their eighties who lived less than a mile away from us. Rain came in through chinks in the roof with alarming regularity. They had seven tins to catch the rain in the kitchen and five in the bedroom. On a bad night the kettle froze on the stove.

There is a very fine line to be drawn between stifling initiative and allowing people to perish. It is the difference between a hand-out and a hand-up. I would have liked a people's state where disabled people like myself would be seen not as an inconvenience but as creatures of innocence, goodness and beauty, meriting the same dignity and respect as the high and mighty. But deep down, I knew it was just a pipe-dream. Since the beginning of time, might was always right. Nothing has changed in the interim. All that has changed is that the victory of the strong is achieved more subtly. Hard currency has taken the place of weapons and brute strength.

At this stage I had grown immune, or thought I had, to my relatives' inimical conversation. Again I was proved wrong. My ears were ringing one day as I left the church, having overheard some of the remarks passed about me by some of my 'close friends'. One of the terms they used in connection with me was 'the actress'. It was said not as an insinuation, but as a simple statement of fact. This woman's inhuman insolence reached us like a communal electric shock. I bit my lip as I looked around for a place to hide.

I had learned Pádraic Pearse's line in school:

*'The beauty of the world hath made me sad.'*

I thought to myself what an idiot he must have been. There were so many things to be sad about, but surely the world's problem was the lack of beauty. Ugliness and cruelty seemed to be pervasive forces. But I put those thoughts out of my mind. Here I was, seething with anger at people judging me, while having the temerity to do the same to Pearse. It was totally irrational to feel angry at him. The problem was with my contemporaries. To be different in Ireland was apparently a criminal offence.

When I came home and told Jimmy, he put his arms around me. In that simple movement he shattered the spell of gloom. He had a marvellous capacity to inseminate joy into my life when I was at my lowest.

Many of my friends and relatives saw *only* a 'disabled' woman. Jimmy saw a precious jewel. The very word 'disabled' was all that needed to be said. It was not just a descriptive term but an evaluative one. When the term 'disabled' was used, a judgement had already been formed. It was an education for me into the potentially destructive power of words, or more precisely into the power of labels. Even more fundamentally, it was an indictment of the shadow of prejudice and ignorance.

My situation called for empathy, not pity. But, at best, people offered Jimmy pity: pity for my condition and pity for my children who had to suffer for my affliction. They saw me as a problem to be endured. Jimmy pitied those who had just an ordinary wife. His was special in his eyes – a magical mixture of mayhem and mystery, mischief and maverick, meekness and mirth, motion and mono-chrome, motley and mild. His words not mine! He would not have swapped me for an Olympic champion or nuclear physicist.

Jimmy was my beacon. He was totally trusting – except when he was given misleading advice from medical people. He seemed to have no idea of the notions of evil or dishonesty. He loved without precondition or qualification. He drew love from me like a magnet and radiated love to his family like an open fire. He was the heart of the family. Although he would never do anything 'miraculous', he produced little miracles in all of us by awakening the good in us all. In regard to my disability, familiarity can destroy contempt just as effectively as it can breed it. Jimmy was the quintessential conduit of kindness of thought, word and action.

When the disparaging comments became too much, I took refuge by thinking over happy memories like the birth of my children. For me, the new baby reflected God's schema of a new life to fill the void of every death and signified a new happier dawn. The baby offered a sign of God's succour and even honour. At the hour of my greatest need, God's generous spirit was gifting us with a new wonder. The chief mourners would at last have cause to rejoice. The baby was a holy vessel from the one who existed before time. God had tested me, but had acted swiftly to restore the disorder. In my eyes, pain was a purgatorial experience to prepare me for the miracle of new life.

As with my pregnancies, both my children had been particularly difficult births. And I was very intimidated by the nurses, even more so by the doctors. They talked an alien language – 'epidurals', 'anaesthetic', 'breast is best', 'X-ray' and 'operation theatre'.

But after, I proudly showed off my new treasures. I had often visited people in hospital, but a maternity ward was a different world, a palace of tenderness and chaos. Studying my new baby was incredibly exhilarating. I marvelled at his tiny, chubby face, with his constantly changing expressions, his minuscule hands and fingers swinging around like a bicycle wheel and his round, demanding tummy.

I stroked Anthony's silky hair with great caution, afraid that he would either bite me or that his head might roll off if I touched him too hard. As I relaxed, though, I thought that nothing had ever been so soft and fine. His little mischievous smile enthralled me. Time stood still while he smiled. As I was discovering my new son, there was a protracted discussion going on between my mother, aunts and relatives as to whom Anthony took after.

'He is like his great uncle.'

'Not at all. He is not on that side of the family. He is more like his great-grandfather.'

'I don't think so. He is more like his first cousin in America.'

'What are ye talking about? He is the cut of his father.'

No branch of the family tree was ignored.

## Hope Springs Eternal

Regularly Jimmy brought me for a check-up, before and after my diagnosis. From time to time he would have to bring me to a specialist in the hospital. I would come home from every second such excursion with news of new treatment or medical advances in America which might benefit me. This raised my hopes, but hope is a double-edged sword. None of the family were naive enough to expect a miracle but they all hoped and prayed devoutly that a way would be found for me to have a decent quality of life. That dream insulated us from feelings of total despair. We never had great expectations, but we had little dreams. Hope, though, can build you up only to knock you down. Every time the glimmer of a possible improvement was held out to me something happened to slam the door of optimism into my face. Dreams were an essential but risky investment.

The frenetic pace and continuous worry were taking their toll on me. My face appeared to be getting more haggard and distraught every day. Physically, psychologically and emotionally, I was on the brink. At times Jimmy feared I was on the verge of a nervous breakdown. I was far too young to look so old. In brief periods of remission my spirits were transformed. Over those few weeks it was noticeable to all my family that I smiled more, seemed less edgy, my shoulders drooped less obviously and I no longer seemed to be carrying the weight of the world on my back.

## Close Encounters of the Medical Kind

Events took a turn for the better with another change of house as our family made the short journey to Ferbane in 1978. My drooping spirits were revitalised by an encounter with the local doctor, the late Dr John Cuddigan. There had been too many moments of utter humiliation and abandonment and these left a scar which would take a long time to heal. Meeting a sympathetic doctor like Dr Cuddigan was the first stage in my rehabilitation. For years I had suppressed feelings of blind rage – of feeling little more than a creature to be examined, a bed number, at worst an annoyance. My defences had not just been breached, they had been destroyed.

After a couple of visits, Dr Cuddigan remarked that I was very nervous and afraid of doctors. He asked me why was that the case and told me that I had nothing to fear, because no doctor has a right to make a patient feel stupid.

What I found most reassuring was his insistence that there was always a reason why a patient felt pain – either physical or mental. I was thus saved from drowning in a sea of self-pity. For the first time in years I felt a faint stirring of the self-confidence that I needed to admit to the outside world that I was in pain and that there was nothing to be ashamed of when I was unable to manage my work around the house for weeks at a time.

I did not realise it at the time, but the family's sojourn in Ferbane coincided with a period of slight remission for a few years and I was able to move reasonably freely with the help of a stick. However, as was so often the case, just as one problem was abating a new one was casting its shadow. This time the problems were with my womb. With much fear and foreboding I embarked on another whirlwind tour of visits to doctors, hospitals, X-ray departments. Again, for a long time I found it difficult to reconcile myself with the apparently casual, 'Oh there's nothing to worry about. Go home and pull your-self together.' An interaction with one particular doctor was very distressing.

Eventually I was forced to have a hysterectomy. Unfortunately the operation did not solve all my problems and I was quickly back to regular visits to the hospital. At first, I was very disappointed that surgery had not helped, but it made life more manageable. Later I would conclude that, on balance, the operation had been worthwhile, believing that when a promised banquet turns out to be simply a good meal it is important to remember that, after all, it was a good meal.

Reading my journal of the entire period now, one of the saddest parts is that I so often describe myself in the language of failure. Again and again, it was agony, facing doctors who were often too busy to give me the understanding and sympathy I craved. The tone is one of deep desolation. Surprisingly, though, there are also flashes of warmth, moments when I seem to sense that someone – who, at a moment in history almost two thousand years earlier, had even been more wretched and lonely – was with me in a very special way. Nothing could shake that solid rock of faith. The words reveal a tale of poverty and riches. For all their simplicity, they evoke the drama of the gospel in a modern incarnation. The vocabulary is one of suffering.

In my journal, there is a personal account of pain and death being intertwined with resurrection. I do not use images to describe my pain, but the feeling is reminiscent of Gerard Manley Hopkins' image of his life as a shipwreck. One windy day shortly before the end of his own life, he has a vision of sunlight coming into the turmoil of a summer storm. This led to one of his finest works when he is acutely aware of the sense of unity with Christ Risen, an image of himself as no longer a poor joke of a wasted life, but someone precious, just like hidden treasure discovered in a shipwreck. Despite my discontent with the prejudice against me and the extent of my suffering, I too retained an overwhelming sense of joy and celebration at my own dignity because of my closeness to the Holy Family.

In 1983, five years after being diagnosed as suffering from MS, I moved back to Athlone with my family. There I became a patient of Dr Patrick O'Meara. After many unhappy encounters with doctors, I was delighted with his attitude just as I'd been with Dr Cuddigan.

I found that Dr O'Meara did not talk above me or down to me, but spoke to me as a person and later as a friend when I got to know him. I still did not talk much about my MS as, by this time, I was having good and very bad days. I knew then there was no cure for MS, so why annoy a doctor about it?

By 1984 the period of remission was long past. In the course of a visit to Galway hospital I was informed about a new 'wonder drug' that was guaranteed to improve my condition in the short term, but which might have side effects. I decided only to take it as a last resort.

Then, by 1986, a marked deterioration in my condition had occurred. I found herself falling more and more frequently. As far as possible I kept these misadventures to myself unless I hurt myself badly in the fall. I was unsure how Jimmy would respond to news of all this falling over and I did not want to cause him extra worry so I continued to bottle all that inside me.


*Omega Point*

I became an expert at the art of subterfuge and concealment, hiding all manner of misfortunes from my family. Eventually I saw the dangers in concealing so much from them.

Things came to a head in 1988. I had been using the stick for a long time – when going out and about, but I also used it in the house when there was no one there to see me. One day in March, while walking with it, I fell and would have been in the fire only the fireguard saved me. This really frightened me. I got my next-door neighbour to bring me to the doctor. For the first time I told him the real truth of my condition and the way I was falling all the time. He put me on crutches and that helped me for a while.

I managed the crutches for about two weeks until one day I found that both my legs were giving me a lot of pain and they both seemed unsteady. I stayed in bed that day. In the afternoon I got up to go to the bathroom and found I could not walk. I fell on the floor. I managed to phone my husband. He came home and told me to stay in bed and rest.

That night, Jimmy was outside. I got up and fell. My son tried to pick me up again, but I couldn't feel my legs. He got his dad and then, when Jimmy came and helped, he fetched the wheelchair and they put me in it. Jimmy seemed to accept the chair better than I did; I was very upset. The next morning Dr O'Meara came to see me. I cried a lot. I felt I had failed because I had not fought my illness adequately. It took me a week or so to realise it was not my fault I was in the chair.

From then on, I never seemed to have a chance with the MS.

Having seen the extent of my pain and distress, Dr O'Meara arranged for me to stay in Athlone hospital. This stay was different from all the others for two reasons. Firstly, my own doctor visited me frequently and took personal care to check my treatment and keep me informed of all that was happening to me. It was a novel experience for me to feel totally relaxed in a hospital. The fact that my nursing staff were very attentive and sympathetic to me made me feel very much at home. It was reassuring to know that these people were not just professionals, they were friends.

Secondly, I was no longer able to conceal the gravity of my condition. I had so successfully mastered the art of concealment that even Jimmy did not notice that I had lost so much power in my hand that I had great difficulty eating. My speech was becoming progressively more slurred. When this was discovered in the hospital, Jimmy was told immediately. It was a very traumatic experience for him.

Jimmy found it hard to take at first and blamed the hospital until my doctor explained things to him. In one way it was a relief that they found out at home about how bad things had become. I did not have to hide it from them any longer. I found that I had great support and understanding from my family and now I trusted my doctor with my life. I was not afraid of being pushed around. I felt that if I kept up my spirits up, things would not get worse – but that was wishful thinking on my part.

The next twelve months were a further chapter in my decline. It reached a stage where it was impossible for me to pick up anything. I got a kidney infection that lingered for months. For the first time the muscles in my throat started acting up to the extent that I felt I was choking all the time. Things reached rock bottom.

By August 1989, I found I could no longer hold my head straight. I had to wear a collar around my neck. I was told to wear it at night as well as in the daytime. I was passing blood. My bowels were not functioning properly and I had to be cleaned and washed. I felt so sick from infection and pain that I could no longer take any interest in my family.

I was at the stage where I had no dignity left. MS had taken that.

# 8

# Miracle

*'This thou perceiv'st, which makes thy love more strong,*
*To love that well, which thou must leave ere long.'*

— WILLIAM SHAKESPEARE, 'Sonnet 73'

On a drab and uninspiring evening in August 1879, a small community witnessed an apparition at Knock, through sheets of driving rain and howling wind. The visitation gave hope to a famine-struck and persecuted region. Today, pilgrims continue to flock to the shrine at Knock.

The Blessed Virgin is both awe-inspiring and an intimate friend. The oldest pilgrims are devout and sad — wondering will they be alive to make the trip next year. Many pilgrims are armed with flasks, mustard-laden ham sandwiches and raincoats. Some have travelled by train via Claremorris station. The station is done up in blue and white, the traditional colours of the Virgin. The stampede for the bus to the shrine is like a scene from the Battle of the Alamo. The first impression is of a row of cars and hedges — the car registrations are often from each of the thirty-two counties of Ireland, with plenty of continental cars in their midst. The traditional hawkers have been displaced to the more slightly purpose-built side where people can engage in business or drink the soup of secularism depending on one's point of view. Tourists purchase the obligatory holy water bottle and chat amiably to the stall owner.

Stewards decked out in bright green sashes direct the teeming crowds like traffic police. One man jokes that he is seeking a cure for baldness. A distraught lady praying to give up cigarettes is horrified to discover herself trying to light a fag with the same match she used to light a candle in the grotto.

A baby sleeps in the corner. She is two weeks old, a pale little thing with blue eyes set in a small face. Her face is drenched in sweat and the blue towel near her head is quite wet. The baby's hands jerk convulsively outside the tiny blanket. She looks pathetically small in the bed, a tiny martyr in the grip of illness. The baby's mother looks terribly afraid.

She kneels beside the cradle. In the stillness, there is a noble humility about her kneeling figure. So still is she that she looks like a statue called out of darkness itself. As if transfixed, she stares at the little face, still deadly pale despite the thick coat of sweat. Suddenly the baby's eyes open wide and nothing has ever seemed so huge as those blue jewels. She stares at her mother, as if sensing her concern. Almost in spite of herself, the mother looks deep into the depths of her baby's eyes and knows that this child is suffering a great deal. The fragile little hands open and close as if registering arrows of pain shooting through her frail body.

But now, she smiles at the baby and in that moment the fellow-ship of the besieged is clearly established. Her patience seems infinite. Time does not matter, for her it doesn't exist. In her eyes, the universe is centred in that child so small she scarcely ruffles the blankets. She sits beside the baby, listening to her breathing, feeling her body twitch slightly as her restless mind flees through the corridors of her dreams. Occasionally she strokes her forehead.

So delicately light is her touch, her fingers scarcely seem to fondle the baby's fingers when they touch. They are like frail fingers of gossamer brushing her tiny hands. Her vigil of love continues. In this sea of suffering, love and despair sink to new depths and soar to new heights.

Some pilgrims seem soaked in a heavy despondency as if some totally melancholy spirit broods over the place. Illness is sucking the vitality out of many victims as a bee sucks honey out of a flower. The basilica is a monument to broken hearts and foiled aspirations, to innumerable tales of sadness and dawning shreds of hope.

The badly faded memory of a line I had learned in school from a poem by Yeats came to me as I recoiled from the suffering which some people existed in:

'*For the world's more full of weeping than you can understand.*'

A person, it is held, can become accustomed to anything, but suffering for these people is a recurring nightmare. Often, during severe illness, it is difficult not to succumb to a great sense of the desolation of life which sweeps all round like a tidal wave, drowning all in its blackness. The real miracle of Knock is that the black clouds are lifted – at least temporarily. The most frequent healing is on the inside.

To look behind the faces of some of the people is to discover the harshest realities of human existence. They are searching the hidden places of the mind for the elusive memory of overwhelming happiness. Most are there for the anointing of the sick. Wheelchairs are lined up almost in military style and priests in white robes with blue crosses anoint them with oil held by handmaidens. The pilgrims are clearly heartened by this attention and blessing. Inside the bright, celestial blue basilica a wonderful choir sings inspiring messages.

## Hallowed Be Thy Name

'Every cloud has a silver lining' – at least according to the old maxim. I was to experience the truth of this saying through my illness which focused my attention and altered my perspective on life. In the hurricane of emotions I went through when confronted by death, God became a personal God rather than someone abstract and distant.

A few years ago, while on retreat, Fr Gearoid O'Conaire, a Franciscan priest who served at Athlone, noticed a spider, which, over the course of several days never seemed to move. He imagined she was dead, until one day a fly touched off the web and, like a bolt of lightning, she pounced, although this time unsuccessfully. For Fr Gearoid, this experience encapsulated what it means to be a contemplative in action. The contemplative person waits for the appropriate time to act and to act in a way that is consonant with what is right just at that moment. This helps the person develop a new way of being in the world; a new lifestyle, as well as a new way of acting, particularly non-violently. It appears that many initiatives come into being more from personal needs than led by the Holy Spirit. It is a reminder that, when you least expect it, and are feeling very low, God can burst into your life.

The knowledge that I could have died, that I had to assess my performance in life, produced in me a very real desire to live, if God willed it. I felt that I still had something to contribute to my family. I think that my own particular religious faith, which is strongly grounded in the love of God and the Holy Family and in the hope which springs from this love is what kept me going. I felt that the Holy Family was a guiding hand and, in that way, my general attitude and approach to what should be done was much better attuned to dealing with real priorities.

One of the benefits to me of the illness has been that it has intensified this personal relationship to a remarkable extent. Until then God tended to be somebody remote to whom I gave orthodox prayer and to whom I paid homage at Mass. As I talked to God during my illness in a more personal way, I began to develop an even more intimate relationship with Him.

I often think that it must be very difficult to achieve peace without prayer. Prayer was my great buttress during my illness; it was from prayer that I got hope and confidence. This is enormously important when you are lying on your bed all day, because it gives you the right psychological attitude to a serious illness. There are two sides to it; the practical and the spiritual. But it all stems from a resurrection of the human spirit fortified by belief in the love of God.

The Bible tells us: 'I can do all things in Christ who strengthens me.'

I believe that the truth these affirmations express is powerful for one's self confidence and that it can pull you out of the depths of difficulty and despair.

In the words of St Paul: 'He who believes in God can surmount any heights or depths.' To believe in the power of God is, in my view, a very important anchor to have because it enables one in time of tribulation to survive and to fight against the very real difficulties that would otherwise cause one to despair.

While I never totally despaired, I was close to it on many occasions. Then, when I went back to be fortified by the Holy Family, the confidence that this gave me helped me to feel that nobody could be against me or beat me if He was on my side. I believed that God was on my side. This was a tremendous source of strength during my illness.

I think that my suffering also helped me to focus my attention on my relationships. I think I've always been people-orientated in terms of getting on with people, but it certainly helped heighten my perception of, and gave greater meaning to, my relationships, particularly with my husband and family. The enormous sustenance which they were to me during that particular period made a great impact on our family. It has also helped in my relations with people in general.

The two poles of my emotional state at this time are evident in every sentence in my journal as I recall those months; the scream and the whisper, the tumult and the gentleness, the loud exhortation and the protective veil – all arising from my own inner turmoil and my love for the family.

I feel that my whole human spirit needed to be lifted and I don't think I could have lifted it on my own. Having the Lord with me was an enormous help in taking me away from the brink of despair. At all times I prayed that whatever His will decreed, I would offer myself on that basis. And if it would be His will that I survive, well then I would do my best to justify that decision on His part.

Yet there were times when my faith flagged. It is not easy to always look on the bright side of life when you know you are dying. I knew that a local chaplain had even begun to write the homily for my funeral.

The Gospels are full of Good News – God's love for us, hope, life, wisdom and truth. I was able to discover a great happiness and peace within myself because God was there, patiently waiting with open arms for me. It's the type of feeling described by Job. As he tells us, God is the silence, a voice that speaks without words, a quiet that is loud with conviction, the calm at the centre of a storm.

I took strength, too, from knowing others could help me somehow by praying for my body and soul. This was a bed-rock Catholic tradition, based on an unshakable belief in the mercy of God, a belief which predated Christianity and received its first expression in Judas Maccabeus.


## A Day Out

Surprisingly, given my few opportunities for any kind of social outings, I was not all that keen to travel to Knock when the opportunity arose.

Even so, when Gerry Glynn, of the Order of Malta in Athlone, asked me would I go to the shrine at Knock, I said I would go anywhere to get away from the four walls. It didn't mean too much to me. I thought it was a cold and barren place. The last time I was there, it was lashing rain and there was a gale blowing. That day, too, we found trouble getting hold of a wheelchair. That time, I thought it was the most miserable place and we didn't even wait for the Mass before we got in the car and went home. I'd made a promise to myself that as long as I lived I wouldn't be caught dead in the place again. The shrine at Lourdes was always my favourite place. I had really wanted to go to Lourdes in 1989, but my illness was so expensive we couldn't afford the trip.

When Gerry asked me to go to Knock, I knew I was very sick, I knew I didn't have long to live; I really didn't want to go because I had been praying to Our Lady and Our Lord to let me live long enough to see Cora and Anthony out of their teenage years, but I knew that wasn't going to be. In the end, the trip appealed to me because a day out of the house would give Jimmy a break from looking after me.

The morning began as all my mornings began, with Jimmy gently shaking me by the shoulder. I was not a great riser, especially since the illness had reached crisis point. I loved the heat beneath the cotton sheets and blankets and hated having to venture onto the cold floor and retrieve my clothes. Worse still was the coldness which attacked me when I got up.

It was around this time that I'd noticed a change in Jimmy. The lines on his face had become more accentuated. He looked to be suffering from a bout of perpetual tiredness, as if most of his energy had been stolen. Although he was only a young man, it occasionally appeared that Father Time had caught up with him prematurely. His mood was more melancholic. I resolved to pray for him harder than ever.

When we got to Knock, they brought me on my stretcher to the nurse and she settled all the usual things you do with an invalid. I was too sick to be brought to the basilica immediately, so I was taken to the rest and care centre. Eventually, just before Mass, we went over to the basilica and they put me under the statue of Our Lady of Knock. When I looked up at the statue, that's the statue they carry in the procession, I thought she was the most beautiful and friendliest statue I had ever seen in my life.

I had been thinking about dying, about Jimmy, Cora and Anthony. I knew, being a young mother, that people would give Cora and Anthony an extra bit of love and attention, but I was worried about Jimmy because we were only married for three months when I got sick, and he'd built his whole life around me. I mean, he could have run out on me because all of a sudden he was caught every way; he was caught mentally, physically and financially. He was very quiet, he never went out with the lads. If he wasn't at work he was with me, that's the way we were. If a woman loses her husband everyone supports her, if a man loses his wife they think after two days he's all right. But there's no difference. I knew that when the funeral was over people would think he didn't want anybody or need anybody.

I was thinking if Jimmy was the one to die on me how I would feel in myself. There would be part of me gone. When there's part of something gone, it's hard to make it whole again.

These were the thoughts and feelings that were going around in my heart and mind, but I couldn't put them into the words I wanted. I wanted another housewife, another woman to talk to me who would understand what was within me, and I looked back up at the statue of Our Lady and I said to her, 'You are a mother, too; you know how I feel about leaving my husband and children.'

It wasn't a prayer, it wasn't a statement, it was just one woman chatting to another. I then prayed to her to look after Jimmy and the children and to give them the grace to accept my death as the will of God.

The Rosary was recited and Benediction imparted, and when the bishop walked down with the Eucharist during the blessing of the sick and came to the front of my stretcher, I heard the words: 'The lame shall walk.' When the ceremonies started, my bishop anointed me. After I was anointed, I got restless. I can't explain it. It was really my mind that was restless. I can't really explain this, but when it came to the consecration during Mass, I wasn't afraid but all of a sudden I wanted someone I knew near me. I received Holy Communion, after which I got a tremendous pain in both my heels, which was very unusual. Then the pain disappeared and so did all the other pains in my body.

After Communion there was the Rosary, Benediction and the Blessing of the Sick. It was at that time that I got this magnificent feeling – a wonderful sensation like a whispering breeze telling me that I was cured. I got this beautiful, magnificent feeling telling me that, if the stretcher was opened, I could get up and walk. Being very practical, I laughed the feeling off.

My mind was a tangle of thoughts: orderless, confused, inexpressible. I tried to cop myself on and remind myself that I was going to die. I knew that if I said to anybody to open the stretcher they would get a nurse and I knew the nurse would say, 'No, she's too sick, just pacify her.' So I decided I would tell nobody and that I would go home and tell Jimmy, because Jimmy always sorted things out for me.

I was last out of the basilica and I looked up at the Statue of Our Lady and I said to her, 'Well, if you did do anything for me in Knock and I didn't tell anybody, maybe by the time I got to Roscommon you might take it back.' I was trying to laugh it off. My friend Nuala came over to talk to me and I couldn't control myself and I said to her, 'Would you think I was stupid if I said to you that if the stretcher was opened I could get up and walk?' And she said no, but I knew the poor woman didn't know what to say, so she called a nurse who opened the stretcher and my two legs swung out and I stood up straight.

It was the first time in three years I had been able to do so. I wasn't a bit stiff even after all those years. Not forgetting that I'd been strapped into the stretcher since quarter to nine that morning and this was half-four in the afternoon, and you know even because of that I would have expected to be stiff. I got a lovely warm feeling and it has stayed with me constantly ever since.

I am absolutely convinced it was a miracle.

My speech was perfect and my hands and arms were perfect. I was standing unaided on my own two feet. I spoke normally to Nuala and was holding my head up straight without support.

## A Moment of Grace

Standing there that moment, I saw my own heart right in front of me. And it was so full of joy and peace and love without end and it was shining. It was like looking directly into the sun and then the rays came towards me and I received all these gifts of joy and peace and love, and a lot of other things.

Mrs Coyne, the chief handmaiden in Knock, put me sitting down and she gave me *The Knock Annual*. The book opened as Mrs Coyne handed it to me, and I, who had been almost blind, read clearly: 'Why is the Rosary so powerful?' Then I said to Mrs Coyne, 'That's our prayer, that's the prayer of our home and family.'

They gave me a cup of tea and I had it nearly finished when I realised I had held the cup and saucer in my hands, something I hadn't been able to do for years. At this stage, everyone was by now getting a bit excited.

I sat up straight the whole way home in the ambulance. I wouldn't even lean back. I was walking down the steps of the ambulance and Jimmy was bringing the wheelchair around.

He said, 'Well, how was Knock?'

I said, 'Ah, it was all right, Jim. Sure why would anybody bother going down there.'

He hadn't realised that I was walking. So I stood up at the patio doors and I said, 'Look, Jim, I can walk.'

'Oh God, Mar,' he said, 'don't...'

I went over and put my arms around him and I never saw a man crying like that. He just got down on his knees and started thanking the Lord. The full scale of all that he suffered over the previous seventeen years really became apparent. A lot of tears were shed in our house that day.

My greatest moment that day was walking over and putting my arms around my daughter to feel her in my arms and let her feel my love instead of trying to tell her.

Then my son, Anthony, came in and saw all the commotion.

When I told him I could walk he said, 'Oh, yeah,' and ran out again, only fully appreciating what had happened when he told his friends.

I was home three days from Knock when I got a little time to myself from all the excitement that was going on in my house and I realised first of all that I had received Holy Communion normally at Knock, which I hadn't been able to do in a long time – I used to have difficulty swallowing and would have to take a lot of drink when I received it. I thought about the pain in my heels coming and going, and when that went every pain in my body went with it.

That was the last time I knew pain. I hadn't known life without pain since 1972.

## The Morning After

However, in the immediate aftermath of my cure, I was not to know if my 'miracle' would last or not. I now entered a new world of temporary, acute anxiety.

The next morning we didn't know what to do. We decided to behave as normally as possible. Jimmy went to work, Cora went to school. My nursing home help came in. I let her wash and dress me and put me in the wheelchair. The doctor came during the day and I told him about the trip to Knock and then I stood up and walked a few steps.

'I don't know. Something wonderful has happened,' he said. 'You were very sick on Friday, what do we do now?'

I said, 'I don't know. This never happened to me before.'

'Well!' he said. 'It never happened to me before either.'

So we decided to play it by ear and carry on as before. I had a marvellous day sitting up in the bed, and then going out for a drink of water just for the fun of it. But by Tuesday I was getting fed up. The nurse came in and I ran over to her and I ran back to the bed.

On Wednesday I went to the physio and when the doctor came in I stood up and walked around feeling very proud of myself.

We only told my parents, relatives and doctor of my cure. I didn't want it turned into a circus. I had lived the life of a disabled person for seventeen years. It was quite difficult to adjust to living a normal life again. In fact, I suffered from a mild form of depression for a few weeks, as I tried to cope with life as an ordinary housewife and mother. It was only through prayer and jotting down a daily rota of chores for myself that I was able to come to terms with it.

The funny part was that the muscles were wasted on my legs for a very long time, but when I came back from Knock they were perfect. I still had a catheter in – and that was a potential problem because when you have a catheter in for a long time there's a good chance you'll need an operation.

Nobody knew what to do because this had never happened before, and so it was a fortnight before they decided to take it out. The morning the nurse came, she said she would take it out and that if I got into trouble she would come back and put it in. So I was sitting in the bed wondering if this part of me is working, and if this part of me isn't working, and if this part doesn't work is the other part a miracle? So I prayed the Rosary. I always pray the Rosary when I don't know what to do. After about twenty minutes or so I jumped out of the bed, turned on the tap in the sink in the bedroom and I ran to the toilet. I never used the catheter again and I've never had a kidney infection since. I've never looked back.

In many miracle cures, doctors are unable to explain what has happened. Medical opinion tends to be split into two camps. Sceptics claim that the original diagnosis was wrong or that the problem was psychological.

The Knock Medical Bureau, whose function it is to establish

Baby Marion on the wall of her local school.

Marion prepares to blow out the candle on her cake at her first birthday party.

Marion on the day her brother makes his first Holy Communion.

Marion with grandad Jimmy Finglas.

Marion in Scotland with her grand-aunt Finglas.

The teenage Marion in Athlone.

Jimmy (left) on peacekeeping duty in Cyprus.

Jimmy on honeymoon.

Love Changes Everything. Marion and Jimmy's wedding day.

Marion with Cora and
Anthony the first Christmas
after her cure.

Cora, Anthony and Marion
in Blarney.

Marion with Cora and
baby Chantel on
Ellis Island.

Maureen (Marion's mother), Marion, Anthony
and Cora at Anthony's passing-out.

Marion at a family gathering.
Back: David (brother), Anthony , Joe (father-in-law)
and Jimmy. Front: Maureen (mother), Marion,
Jacinta (sister) and Cora.

Daisy and Joe Carroll with
Ena Slevin.

Silver Bells. Marion and Jimmy
celebrate their 25th anniversary.

Jive Talking. Marion and
Jimmy on the dance floor.

Marion and Jimmy on holiday in Egypt.

Marion in Fátima, Portugal.

Marion in America with cousin Jim Carroll (left), and a friend.

Marion and Jimmy as guests on radio in New York.

Marion goes to Graceland!

Jimmy, Sister Briege McKenna, Marion and Father Kevin Scallon.

A Papal Blessing. Marion receives Holy Communion from Pope John Paul II in Rome.

Marion with Gerry and Ann Flanagan, and a friend.

And so this is Christmas! Jimmy in his new role as Santa's ambassador.

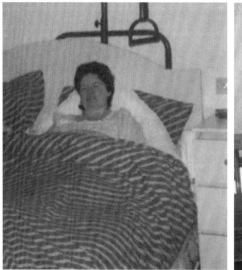

The Lowest of the Low. Marion in her sick bed before her cure.

Marion with the Mayor of Sligo at a civic reception for her after her cure.

Cora, Marion and Jimmy in Knock.

Marion greeting her mother,
as a handmaid in Knock.

Margaret Hattie makes a
presentation to Jimmy and Marion
on a visit to Scotland.

Marion on *Kenny Live* with Pat Kenny.

Ceremony. Marion with the late Bishop Dominic Conway at the statue of
Our Lady for the Marian year in Lough Key Forest Park.

Marion with Mother Teresa in Knock in 1993.

Marion speaks at the Rosary Rally in Knock.

Hotel Paradise. With the staff of the Knock House Hotel.
From left: Brian Crowley (general manager), Lorcan Vale (assistant manager), Derek and Thomas (chefs),
Jimmy, Rosin and Laura (restaurant staff), and Marion.

Marion with the stewards and handmaids in Knock.
They have been a massive support to Marion down the years.
Back from left: John Hynes, Bernie Cummins, Mary Gibbin, Anne Marie Duggan Hayes, Jimmy.
Front from left: Bridie Hughes, Catherine Hynes, Marion, Margaret Kilcumin, Mary Gaughan, Breege Griffin.

Marion blesses a nun.

Magic Moments. Marion and
Jimmy, during the ceremonies in
Knock in 2019.

Sharing the Joy. Bishop Colm O'Reilly extends his good wishes to Marion
after the big announcement in Knock.

Quiet Satisfaction. Marion savours the moment after the announcement of her miracle cure at Knock.

Oh Happy Day. Bishop Francis Duffy congratulates Marion at the announcement of her official cure in Knock.

Walk Tall. Marion takes part in the procession at the ceremony at Knock.

whether or not a miracle took place, subsequently launched an investigation into my case. Their deliberations consider three criteria:

1. The cure must be sudden.
2. The cure must be complete, i.e. there must be no residual manifestations of the illness.
3. The cure must be maintained for a number of years.

My own doctor, Dr Patrick O'Meara, did not accept that my cure was a remission. Remissions normally occur over a period of time, and not to such a scale as that which happened to me.

## A New Dawn

Life after my miracle cure was, for me, one of readjusting to the simple things of life. After so long suffering from a crippling illness, the ordinary was extraordinary to me.

A few days later, on a frosty morning, I woke before the others and went to get the briquettes from the shed. The ground was silvery white and the clothes stiff on the washing line. I reached to feel the clothes, and my hands stuck to them. I felt them again and again, watching the hands that had not worked for years move again, experiencing the sensation of touch, my warm hands on the cold, clean clothes. I sauntered down the path, stood to look back at the tracks my footprints made in the white frost: my own two feet alone, unassisted by crutch or wheelchair. It was a magic moment.

## Why Me, Lord?

In the days after my cure I was to spend much time pondering why God had gifted me with such a wondrous blessing.

I don't feel a responsibility to the Lord. People say to me, 'You must have been a saint.' I wasn't; I could be a holy terror! I was just a very ordinary person. I was doing our family Rosary one night and I said, 'Jesus why me? Everybody is asking me, and I want to ask You.' I got my answer. My cure and my healing in Knock doesn't belong to me, none of it belongs to me. This is a special gift for the people of the world to let everyone know that Jesus is there. We are so human, especially when we are down.

When I was ill, I went through a stage of mourning the things I missed: dancing, going out, all those normal things, clothes, I'd even miss the food that I couldn't eat, and that I'd like to try. I think it's usual to go through a stage of that.

I had never prayed for a cure. That might seem strange but I'd never prayed for it. It's one thing reading it in the Bible, it is another thing when it actually happens. And, if we are all honest with ourselves, we are all afraid to say, 'Come on, Jesus, heal my legs and wasted muscle.' You would be a bit afraid to really challenge Him because even if you have a little bit of faith and it doesn't happen, then it's going to take all you have to hang on.

In my heart, I knew from the very start what this was. Remission in Multiple Sclerosis is not uncommon – but this was no remission. And anyway, my muscles couldn't have been as perfect as they were so quickly. I climbed Croagh Patrick when I wasn't a year cured. I cycled a bicycle a week after I'd been to Knock. All these years later, there has been no turning back, in any way. With MS, remission happens gradually and maybe only partially. This was complete and sudden.

In my experience, some people with disabilities don't always look at the gifts they have. For instance, if someone's in a wheelchair and they say, 'Thanks be to God for my health,' it might be the only time in their lives that they say that. People don't always realise that it is the disabled people who help others. We can hope. The people who are walking and who do not have a disability find it hard and are awkward with us, while we don't find it awkward with them. So really, we have to reach out to them.

I have never changed. I don't feel different from anybody else, that's the part of it I don't understand. If you come into our house and say to the children, 'It's great what happened to your mother,' and they would say yes and then they would look at me and say, 'That's the one that lets a roar at me.' We have never changed. I scrub my own floors. We are very, very normal.

If I don't stay as I am, the ordinary Marion Carroll, if I don't live my life as the wife and mother when I can, when I am not working for the Lord, how can I understand people's problems? The Lord didn't choose me to go out and work for Him by keeping me away from people. He chose me because I was one of them, and it's only through being the same as everybody else and living with them that you can understand their needs, and that you can understand their hurts and their wants. That's what I do. I just live my life. I reach out to people and I try to help them.

My cure is a healing gift from Jesus and Mary; I am an instrument of God's love. Life is so hard sometimes that it's just a reminder that God loves us. Jesus is the doctor. I am the prescription. I'm here to serve.

I work under the obedience of the Church in my two ministries; one of healing, the other families. I have taken the vow of confidentiality and try to ensure that God is presented in dignity, love and respect. I am the conductor of God's love; the only part that I give of myself is time.

Most of us are puppets. We all need to get a sense of the approval of others. Often we are wounded by what others say about us. During my illness, I regularly found myself in that position because of people's attitude to my disability.

Even with all our efforts to be sensitive we do end up hurting people with what we say and what we can do. Hurt can produce in us resentment and anger and will nearly always call on us to practise forgiveness. When someone has hurt us deeply we can find it difficult to forgive them. And yet we know in our hearts that it is the right thing to do; that is the Christian thing to do. God always forgives us, so we too must be willing to forgive those who offend us.

Our children always valued the fact that I would listen to them if I couldn't participate in other ways. They, in their turn, have turned out to be very good listeners too. They have an instinct that enables them to reach out to other people. They still chat to me and relate things that are happening, which I realise is increasingly rare in this day and age. It is a beautiful gift from God.

Our connection grew from how Jimmy and the children took turns at washing me, dressing me and feeding me. And so I have nothing but one hundred per cent praise for the army and the men Jimmy worked with. I appreciate the fact that another job might not have been so understanding. It was only through the good leave that Jimmy got that he was able to do so much for me.

I'll always remember our twenty-second wedding anniversary in 1989, when I was really bad. I had no power in my legs or anything. Jimmy dressed me in my best dress, put on the make-up for me and pushed me in the wheelchair into the Prince of Wales for our anniversary dinner. We had no car then as my illness was costing us so much, but Jimmy pushed me the whole two miles and then mashed up my dinner and fed me.

After my cure I resolved I would do all I could for my husband.

## Happy New Year

I love New Year's Day because of its promise of a new beginning. I decided to forgo my normal practice of making my customary new year's resolution: to give up the unholy and unhealthy trinity of cake, chocolate and crisps. Instead I decided think of Bartimaeus – or maybe more accurately the story of the Gospel passage about him.

Mark's Gospel tells us that Jesus and the disciples were making the journey to Jericho. On the side of the road is a blind beggar, Bartimaeus. This simple man was enthralled by the compassion of God towards people. He was inspired by Jesus because he was someone who brought the compassion of God to people: he was someone who did not judge or condemn. This Jesus was someone who was with people wherever they were, especially those who found themselves on the margins of society. That is why Bartimaeus never fell prey to defeatism. He never lost hope because one day he hoped that Jesus would give him back his sight.

The blind beggar, hearing that Jesus is passing by at that very moment, shouts out to Jesus and asks for healing. The disciples, though, are so focused on reaching their destination that they see Bartimaeus as a burden because he is interrupting their travel plans. Mark tells us that 'they scolded him and told him to be quiet'.

However, Bartimaeus is not easily put off. He shouts out again and asks once more for help. This time Jesus stops to find out what all the shouting is about. He asks the disciples to bring Bartimaeus to him. Somewhat begrudgingly, they do. Jesus asks Bartimaeus what he wants and he tells him that he seeks his sight back. Jesus gives the blind man his vision back and says, 'Go, your faith has saved you.'

The strong faith of Bartimaeus should inspire us in this story. So, too, should the mercy of Jesus. However, it is the actions of the disciples that should really be of interest to us. They were all well-intentioned, just as we are. Yet they missed the big picture as we so often do.

There are two clear dangers for all of us in this story. None of the disciples stopped, as Jesus did. They continued to walk on as if nothing was happening. Although they were physically following Jesus, their hearts were elsewhere. We convince, perhaps even delude, ourselves that we are following Jesus, but the reality is that often our hearts are not open.

The other temptation is to follow what Pope Francis calls 'a scheduled faith'. Yes, we walk with the People of God, but we already have our schedule for the journey: everyone must respect our rhythm and every obstacle is a nuisance because it disrupts our predetermined plans. To the disciples, Bartimaeus was an impediment to the schedule they had set out to follow. In the process they forgot what Jesus had taught them, that those on the margins provide the perfect opportunity to meet God. If we are so committed to slavishly following our own plans we can miss out on the possibilities of meeting Jesus in others.

At the closing Mass of the Synod of the Family, Pope Francis observed:

'In the end, Bartimaeus followed Jesus on the path. He not only regained his sight, but he joined the community of those who walk with Jesus. Let us follow the path the Lord desires. Let us ask him to turn to us his healing and saving gaze, never allowing ourselves to be tarnished by pessimism or sin, let us seek and look upon the glory of God, which shines forth in men and women who are fully alive.'

Bartimaeus made the journey from sight to insight and back to sight. Each new year, I ask that I will have both his sight and insight.

# 9

# In the Family

*'Nothing is so strong as gentleness;
nothing so gentle as real strength.'*

— ST FRANCIS DE SALES

For me, the most difficult section in this book is to write about my
family life. The problem is that to tell the truth, the whole truth and
nothing but the truth, is to leave myself wide open to the accusation
of being mawkishly sentimental – that the description of life in our
household is too good to be true. If only that was the case! If only I
was a domestic goddess like Nigella Lawson! While no marriage or
family unit is perfect, we try to make a valiant attempt to reach the
pinnacle of domestic bliss. I am not saying it is easy for any of us or
that we always succeed! If it sounds almost idyllic then the portrait
fairly represents the reality. However, my family life was not always
so bountifully happy. Illness cast a dark shadow.

Self-pity has no place in my life. I will never accept that I was the
victim of Multiple Sclerosis. Jimmy was. After Knock, there were no
more victims in our family.

Thirty years on from those heady days I still, to a certain degree,
despite my best efforts to the contrary, am wearing the invisible scars
of that experience. As the months passed, I gradually adjusted to life

after my cure, although I was still a long way short of returning to equilibrium. That would have been like putting all the pieces back together after Humpty Dumpty fell off the wall, but I was coping better and returning to a semblance of my old self.

We all live with deep frustrations and broken dreams. Rather than face the incompleteness of our lives and our feelings of loneliness and inner emptiness, we often desperately search for companionship in order to feel a sense of belonging. At the root of much of our restlessness is an impatient waiting for something to fulfil our lives – a marriage partner, power, fame and so on. We refuse to shed dreams that are manifestly not for us. We stand before life with unrealistic expectations. We all seek intimacy and healing in our lives. We seek intimacy because we cannot live without love and affection. We seek healing because we experience sickness and pain. My story is at once universal and particular.

### A Friend in Need ...

I learned quickly who my true friends were, as invariably one does in the hour of crisis. As is so often the case in my moments of need, one person was there for me in my hour of greatest darkness like a lighthouse on a stormy sea – my husband, a well of bottomless generosity.

When the chips were down, as always Jimmy came up trumps. Words cannot adequately express how he helped me in that period and the sacrifices he made, though typical of many husbands, he would never think of it in those terms. Without his support I could never have come through that ordeal. It wasn't so much that he helped me carry on regardless, but somehow he was able to get through those terrible years. I will always be eternally grateful to him for what he did, even though I will never be able to thank him adequately. I can't overstate his importance in my 'rehabilitation'.

Jimmy was my knight in shining armour. While he was gone to work, I just counted the moments until he returned. I will always be in his debt for his unfailing kindness and practical assistance to me during those difficult years.

I vividly remember saying when I was younger: 'Someday I know I'm going to meet somebody and I am going to fall madly in love with him.' Little did I realise at the time that all my prayers would eventually be answered so bountifully. There is definitely someone up there who is watching over us all and things come right in the end. I feel nothing but awe at that recognition.

Sometimes, when I am retelling the story of my cure, my eyes glaze over with the pain of re-living the trauma of the break-up of my body and my illness for the millionth time. Inevitably, when I reach the part about Jimmy I become animated again.

*Crazy Little Thing Called Love*

When Jimmy came into my life, he completely bowled me over. I had no idea I could be consumed with so much love for someone. When Jimmy and I met, we knew, not straight away, but within a short time, that we were right for each other. A typical occurrence when Jimmy's name crops up in any conversation is that my voice habitually softens as I speak of him, assuming an air of deep affec-tion, almost reverence. For all the gentleness there is a great passion and power in his testimony of love. It seems as natural to me to sing Jimmy's praises as to talk about the weather.

He gave me strength when I was weakest. His physical presence alone helped to lift the clouds of darkness around me. My pain was so great that I needed someone there beside me to make me want to keep going. There was a special bond between us, and there still is, but now at last I feel an equal partner again. The quality I admire most in my husband is his patience. He rarely gets cross and always allows the situation to cool down before dealing with a problem. Jimmy and I have great communication. We talk about everything.

Jimmy really enjoys the simple things in life. He gets a great kick out of his family. He can get great pleasure from drinking a cup of tea when he comes home or from pottering around the garden.

## Jimmy

My world is not my world without Jimmy.

If every man is a king of his own castle, then the court of King Jimmy is in a quiet small suburb just outside Athlone, with plenty of greenery and little traffic. The immediate impression is of a good place to bring up kids. The greeting is hardly regal – though always warm and genuine.

The heavy rain and gusting wind can crash against the windows. The dark, sickly sky might close in. Winter will make a defiant last stand despite the coming of summer. But Jimmy is always happy to be seen as he really is. It would not occur to him to put on any pretence. In west of Ireland parlance, he 'has a nice way about him'.

Parenting is a complex business, but my illness posed particular problems for Jimmy. Problems are exacerbated when the one person has to be in some respects both mother and father. It was like landing on an alien planet to begin a new life, with a new language and culture: experiencing poverty, hardships and deprivations; struggling to survive materially, spiritually and emotionally. The deprivations of Jimmy's life were heightened by the fact that I was not really in a position to share his burden – a fact that constantly haunts me.

The practical needs for our family's collective survival dictated that my husband could not wallow in a dull fog of self-pity. My children and I saw him in three roles. There was the provider, often so immersed in work and the business of putting bread on the table that we hardly saw him for the whole day. There was the husband and father, putting on a show for us in public and sparing us his private torment, anxious to give us the right impression, deflecting attention from the enormity of our financial problems to the trivial, using humour to avoid the pain, hiding his feelings even from himself. He continually saved the day with his warmth and optimism, displaying that paternal ability to avoid total despair by smoothing things over, not making a fuss, keeping the peace, preserving the family unit at great personal cost to himself. And, thirdly, there was the suffering man, there in those moments when the mask slipped, and the heartache and grief became too much.

At such times, loneliness was his calling card. There was nothing in it but to endure and carry on. Each new day broke on the world with its own pain and misery. It was like living life trapped in a revolving door. Looking back now, Jimmy realises that it was our love story that was the real story. Ours is a tale of hope and disappointment, joy and sadness, love and the loss of love, effort and despair: the human condition itself, unfolding before our eyes. He watched me grow, turning my potential bitterness into greater depths of love.

I fought a fierce fight to find happiness with a grim determination to avoid emotional disintegration and to cling on to my sense of self and personal integrity. He learned to empathise. It was sad but gripping viewing. Except that for a long time my pain remained. In my subconscious, I felt tearful, frightened, overwhelmed, confused, betrayed; I'd been denied my youth, thrust into middle age before my time. Much of my resentment and anger was denied, though sometimes projected on to God. However, the tie of common blood in our children was not all that truly linked us as man and wife. We both had the same appreciation of life's black humour, the same kindness and sensitivity, and a warm affection for friend and stranger alike.

Jimmy enjoyed passing his few free afternoons working in the garden. He often visited it to be invigorated by its particular silence and mystery. The land had a virginal, unpolluted sacredness that impressed itself silently and directly on him every time he visited it. It had a soul. It was hallowed, it was his holy land.

Before my illness, Jimmy and I had been close, but adversity brought us ever closer together. Our respective needs took different forms, but as colleagues in suffering, our need for healing and companionship was equally great. In succeeding years, our friendship deepened. This taught me something. The lesson I learned was that unhappy and frightening experiences make people emotionally and intellectually humble. It was important to learn how other people coped, to make their insights my own. I could learn from the experience of others. Learning from experience brought some measure of consolation.

## Happiness

My enduring memory of meeting Jimmy for the first time is of an incredibly energetic man, with a radiant smile and a warm voice, and who is totally fulfilled in all aspects of his life. He transmits happiness and inner peace like electricity. He is the perfect tonic for drooping spirits. His vitality is uplifting. To write about his faith would be easy – a much more difficult task is to find words to express the sincerity which is evident in everything he says. His world is amplified to the sounds of respect, integrity and decency.

My own career choice as mother and housewife would not be for every woman, but I have a single-minded devotion to my family. I sometimes have a glow in my face (sometime a frown!) as I go about my tasks in the kitchen these days, still managing to answer a smooth stream of questions from my grandchildren.

When I listen to the conviction in his voice and watch the intense expression that can creep over Jimmy, the inescapable conclusion is that we are made for each other. Jimmy has made a new beginning possible for me since my cure – freeing me largely from my fears and healing my past hurts. He has reached into the centre of my being, enabling me to let go of my anxiety and restlessness and to live fully. Even at the height of my illness, although I was in pain, I felt strangely free when in Jimmy's arms. The ache, the pain, the sadness within his soul over past years is calm now. Peace has at last made a home in my weary heart and mind, too. I have to pinch myself in gratitude for this shared liberation.

We talk for hours and hours about absolutely everything and nothing. Within a very short time after our first meeting we were madly in love with each other. But still I was not going to rush things. My mind is a theatre of happy memories of our 'courting days'. The romance grew like a raging torrent.

Nothing fills the heart like the arrival of a child.

When Anthony was born we were in heaven and our family unit was complete. Cora's birth made it even more perfect.

We don't go out that much, but when we do I just love going out with Jimmy. The next best option from my point of view is a night at home with Jimmy. I wasn't happy going out with my friends unless Jimmy was away on duty. My children are so important to me and I love nothing more than being in the bosom of my family.

Anthony worked initially in hotel management in Christy's,

Blarney, and then in the army in Longford. It was Anthony's child-hood dream to work with the defence forces and we're all delighted that was realised when he got that job.

When Cora was still attending secondary school here in Athlone, it was a great time for both of us. One of the great joys of my life is that we are such great friends. A feature of our life which is particularly close to my heart was our 'girls' night'. When Jimmy and Anthony were working on a Friday night, Cora and I stayed in and rented a video and chatted about everything and anything. From time to time we went on excursions together. A big highlight for both of us was to go together to see Cliff Richard in concert at the Point Depot in 1990. It was only then that I could have afforded an outing like that even as a very special treat.

Sunday nights were for Mick Lally. He decided to pursue a career in teaching, but in 1975 with Garry Hynes and Marie Mullen, he founded the now famous Druid Theatre Company. Two years later he moved to Dublin. He quickly established himself on the stage in Dublin with a string of performances in major productions. However, it was television that made him a household name. After a number of one-off projects, the TV series *Bracken*, the follow-up to the phenom-enally successful *The Riordans*, made Mick Lally a weekly visitor in Irish sitting rooms. *Bracken* was transformed to *Glenroe* and Mick's character Miley claimed a unique affection in Irish people's hearts.

### *What's Love Got To Do With It? Everything*

From the outside, Jimmy and I had some of the appearances of an old-fashioned couple where the husband was expected to be the head of the family, on whom responsibility for its survival depended, the provider, who made all the key decisions. The wife owed not obedience, but acceptance of his decisions. I stayed at home, had the children, looked after them and ran the house. The father was the custodian of order; the mother the catalyst of love and warmth.

But, far from being a hierarchical relationship, our relationship was and is totally egalitarian. We constantly consult one another on everything from the trivial to the crucial, share decision-making and accept an equality of worth. The rising tide of the 1960s in Ireland brought higher material standards. With that people sought higher fulfilment in the next layer of their being such as the areas of emotion and sexuality. The understanding of marriage had subtly changed. Security and peaceful co-existence were not enough. Instead, both partners wanted a relationship of equals in which they were fulfilled by their love. We fitted snugly into this pattern.

Our love was to be seen in two forms. At less cluttered moments – when the children were not under our feet, when we looked at each other in that special way or there was a little furtive touch – we acted then, and still do now, as if we are still falling in love.

Yet we have something which goes much deeper, too. Our communication is exceptional, with Jimmy going against the stereotype of the 'typical Irish man' and as comfortable as me in talking and expressing his feelings. Such is the intimacy of the relationship and our shared desire to know and be known, understand and be understood, express and receive feelings at all times, that more often than not it is impossible to think of us as other than one unit. We try to find a near-perfect balance between closeness and separateness, similar and dissimilar views, dependence and independence. Our greatest gift is empathy. We know intuitively each other's fears, anxieties, insecurities and moods.

This is not to suggest a totally paradisal world – as in every family there are moments of tension. The floor still gets dirty and the dishes have to be washed. We have the same problems as any household.

We just seem to have found the knack of living together in a very happy atmosphere.

## *Rejoice, O Highly Favoured*

Both Jimmy and I are people of strong affections. We knew what we want, and we do not stop wanting it once we have got it. Our mutual admiration remains at honeymoon temperature. Our union celebrates, in a joyous yet sometimes ironic way, the fragile but enduring power of love in a brittle world.

I know that in Jimmy I have found my crock of gold at the end of the rainbow. He gives me the love, security and strength that I didn't believe possible. The highlights of my life, apart from him, are my children. I'm such a lucky woman that he came into my life.

Bliss for Jimmy was to enter the front door after a day's work. Our family was always, and still is, a fixed beam he can hone in upon when he needed to locate himself away from the pressures of his work. He is normally happier with an evening at home than going out. I do enjoy an evening out, but I am not a great party-goer. I derive as much, if not more, pleasure from the 'ordinary world' of family life as I get from the 'extra'-ordinary world of travelling abroad to spread the faith. Cupid's arrow is still at work in our household because we both still worship the ground each other walks on.

The French have a word which has no direct equivalent in the English language – *tendresse*. It describes a love which goes much deeper than physical attraction, something sweet and tender, where consideration is at a premium and when two hearts beat as one. That term could fairly be applied to describe the relationship between us.

I could not have been happier in my marriage after my cure – and it showed.

# 10

# Imagine

*'Abhor what is evil.*
*Hold fast to what is good.'*

— ST PAUL

Although I am now living an active life, I have never forgotten what it was like to be in the throes of a horrifying illness. It was impossible to exorcise the painful memories of what MS has done to me – so much time being unable to move from the neck down, unable to talk, to eat, to go to the toilet. Since my cure I have devoted huge chunks of my time to visiting the sick. I feel a particular responsibility to speak out for disabled people in Ireland.

This is not a new role for me. For ten years prior to my cure, I had campaigned vigorously for the rights of disabled people. People with a great disability are often given a huge cross to carry in life. Equally, though, they are often blessed with many extraordinary gifts – innocence, goodness and an uncanny ability to bring out the best in others.

I myself have known so many such people. In 1988, a year before I was cured, I discovered that I had only very limited power in one of my arms. Consequently I was no longer able to use the standard Mopa wheelchair to move around the house. A group of my former neighbours and friends in Cloghan got together to purchase a much more technologically superior, though very expensive, wheelchair. Our family had acquired huge debts because of my illness and would have been unable to fund such a wheelchair without the help of others. It is a memory I recall with gratitude, because at the time that chair gave me a new lease of life.

Friends of Jimmy's called to see me after I suffered the setback and lost all my power back in 1988. Naturally they were very surprised to find that I was so disabled. They immediately set about raising funds to purchase a wheelchair for me, and the tickets for a function they ran were sold throughout the area in Ferbane, Cloghan, Banagher, Belmount, High Street and Shannonbridge.

Before that I had been an active member of the Athlone Branch of the Multiple Sclerosis Society. I also spent a period as chairperson on the National Fund-Raising Committee in Dublin. In 1985 I was nominated for the Person of the Year awards.

I had been very active up to 1988 when the illness robbed me of the use of my arm. I always found working to raise awareness of MS very challenging – in the best possible way. When I lost the power of my body, I missed the active life I had led up to then. Thanks to the wonderful gesture by Jimmy's friends and others as the organisers of the function to purchase this wheelchair, I had reason to hope that I could live as full a life as possible in the future. That hope was almost as important as the wheelchair itself.

During my illness I wanted to be a champion for people wounded by life, exploited by society, and all those who were marginalised. I wanted to be a bearer of hope, bring joy and meaning to the lives of others. All the time, though, it was my heart that needed healing, my wounds that needed binding because it was me who sometimes felt bereft of hope, crushed like a bruised reed.

## The Voice of the Voiceless

My present-day anxiety to champion the cause of the disabled has its origins in my years spent in the wheelchair. I know both the physical and emotional reality of the problems that people with disabilities face.

There is so much work to be done for disabled people. I am not just speaking about people with MS, but all disabled people. For a person confined to a wheelchair like me, it was almost impossible to gain access to a toilet in the town of Athlone. I am sorry that I have to be so critical, but when I used to take a trip around Athlone in the wheelchair, there were very few places that catered adequately for the disabled or those who needed to use wheelchairs. At the time in Athlone the only two places which catered adequately for wheelchair users were the hospital and the tax office.

As a keen shopper I never find the experience of shopping a chore and am keen to give credit where credit is due – I was very grateful for some of my experiences at the time. Dunnes Stores had a special counter for the disabled and I always found the staff in Quinnsworth first class when I was doing my shopping. I wish I could say the same for other places I was in.

Part of the financial stresses of my illness was that the family had to forgo not just the luxuries of life but many of the basic necessities for a person in my condition. An early casualty of this economy drive was the family car. Since we had no car, we had to rely on public transport a lot. I was a frequent visitor to the Athlone railway station. Like many other stations, facilities for disabled people were almost non-existent. It is fair to say I was less than impressed.

There is a perceptible undercurrent of sadness and anger in people's voices as they relate such incidents to me today. I could sum up their frustration in one sentence, as follows: 'Most of the public buildings in the town as regards the point of access for disabled people are a disgrace.'

Up to the time of my illness, I had taken great pleasure in dancing. This joy was to be another casualty of my MS. There were few opportunities for me to attend musical outings even if Jimmy could have afforded to take me out.

Places of entertainment are very important for all sections of the community. We all need to get out and enjoy ourselves, and, yet again, when I think back to all of the entertainment spots in Athlone, none of them catered for wheelchairs. Being disabled or needing to use a wheelchair does not mean one loses one's appreciation of entertainment. I just love music and, naturally, I would have loved to be able to go out for the odd session, but when the facilities were not there, what else could I do except stay at home?

Another recurring source of irritation to me is the failure of footpaths to encourage disabled people out and about. There are times even now when I would love to paint a big red mark outside all of the premises which are not accessible to the disabled.

Even more galling for me is the lip-service paid to the disabled, which fails to yield any practical benefits. There was so much talk a few years ago about integrating those who are disabled and we heard a lot of mumble about various projects. Yet, so little appears to have been done and it is only when one is sitting confined to a wheelchair that the truth really hits home about the lack of progress in this area. There is so much to be done and I want to fight for a better deal, for all, who are wheelchair users or who are disabled in any other way.

In my time in the wheelchair in Athlone there were at least twenty-five other people in wheelchairs in the area. I would like to see stronger and more effective lobby groups both on local and national levels.

I am convinced that disabled people will have to be more organised in the future. There are organisations in Athlone catering for so many different groups and I feel it would be much better if there was an overall group campaigning for the rights of those people with disabilities. I am talking about the rights to which all citizens of this land are entitled.

Since my cure I have had a burning desire to build more public awareness of the needs of disabled people. All our talking on the subject of disability needs a strong ethical sensibility.

We need to have a voice in the community and our requirements should not be put on the long finger. If God grants me good health, in the future, I am hoping that in my small way I can play a part in securing a better deal for the disabled.

A particular concern is the need to provide a sense of security, especially in the wake of a spate of attacks and robberies on disabled people. When I came home from hospital in 1988 Athlone Lions Club installed a security system in the house again, which was something that was a great asset to my life. Also my wonderful neighbours including my very special friends, Ida Harris and her son, Roger, were my watchdogs during the day. Many disabled people are not so lucky and, as a consequence, live their lives in fear. We all need peace of mind.

The problem is resources, or more precisely lack of resources. Many medical and technological advances have presented new and exciting treatment options – the use of art therapy to help people cope with mental health issues is just one such innovative example. However, there is still a major shortage of funding, which leaves many disabled people seriously disadvantaged.

A number of questions present themselves about the place of disabled people in society today. In Ireland, are all people equal, or are some, like those who are disabled, seen as less equal than others? How many disabled people are institutionalised? How many have a home of their own? How many have access to the special education that they may require? How many have a job that offers fulfilment and meaning to their lives?

One of the buzz phrases today in social and political life is the 'democratic deficit' – the frustration ordinary people have because they are denied any real power in the society they live in, with no say in the decision-making processes. For the disabled person the possibility of making decisions for themselves is often little more than a pipe dream. Decisions about their welfare are often taken by people who have no direct experience of what it is like to be disabled. The balance is shifting slowly, but the reality of active participation by disabled people in plans for their own rehabilitation remains far on the horizon. The need for people to be consulted, and the importance of them being able to express an opinion on the quality of the services made available for them does not seem to be fully appreciated.

## Try a Little Tenderness

In seeking a new deal for disabled people, it is important that this task is complemented with the establishment of adequate support systems for the families of disabled people. Many surveys suggest that there is considerable stress in the families of disabled people, particularly on the children. It has been claimed that the shock of being told that a family member is disabled can feel like being told that she or he has a terminal disease.

Classically, like other forms of grief, there are five stages in this trauma. After the early shock has subsided the first stage of denial begins. The second stage is anger – somebody or something is blamed for the calamity. Bargaining is the third stage where the family might try to do a deal with God, perhaps promising to reform all the darker sides of a person's life in return for a miracle cure. The fourth stage is depression when the person starts to see that the facts are true – the person is disabled and is not going to be 'cured'. The fifth stage, acceptance, is where the family have essentially got to grips with the new situation and resolved it in the best way they can. Such acceptance does not come easily. The magic ingredients for such an outcome are time, care, kindness and sensitivity.

Even worse than the loss of one's physical or mental faculties is the loss of dignity. Shamefully, some disabled people have been made to feel like objects rather than people. I wince at the memory of particular people who did not go out of their way to conceal their animosity towards me.

### Handle My Heart With Love

I was appalled to see that prejudice towards disabled people extended even to Sunday Mass. Some of the most 'upright' pillars of the community would not sit on the same seat as people with disabilities. I thought that there where was a curious irony in coming together to worship and listen to the word of God calling for love of one's neighbour and at the same time deliberately ignoring a real-life neighbour. The eloquence of the words did not translate into practical action.

In later years, the memory of that arrogance was to return to me when reading a story in the newspapers about a wayward minister of the Anglican Church. The then Archbishop of Canterbury, Dr Runcie was asked to comment on the incident. He simply said: 'In this earthly tabernacle there are many mansions and they are all made of glass.' Dr Runcie was highlighting the importance of compassion and sensitivity in human relationships. In the treatment of those with a disability, I had an inkling of the meaning of the saying: actions speak louder than words.

My blood boils when I think of all the indignities disabled people have been subjected to, such as people forced into demeaning conditions in hospitals for the mentally unwell, which were known as 'the madhouse' and 'the human hell'. Such a hospital would generally be an intimidating building: monstrous, ugly, brooding and profoundly sad. It would be full of people with tragic stories like one I heard of a man called Gerry (not his real name), who lost all his cattle herd to TB. Overnight the family faced financial ruin. Gerry was a non-drinker and non-smoker and all his life he'd worked sixteen hours every day. A tall, dapper man he had never hurt anybody in his life, but something inside him snapped when he saw everything he had worked so hard for disappear. He became paralysed with depression and lost the will to live. There was no escape for the pernicious cancer which insidiously ravaged his soul. A black hole within him seemed to be sucking out all his old vitality.

The atmosphere changed in his home. His voice became progressively louder. It betrayed his anger and his inability to cope. For her part his wife Elizabeth (not her real name) became ever more silent. She had run out of soothing platitudes. The only words of comfort she could remember had all been used many times before. Whenever she did that she felt she was closing the door of love, but when he hit the kids she felt her skin crawl. And things reached the point of no return when he began beating his children violently. Each breath his children took used to be a little miracle to him, but it became an irritation. He had to be 'committed'. Elizabeth wondered how her love could turn to such intense hate.

After Gerry was dispatched to the hospital, Elizabeth did not know which was the worst, worrying about the lack of money, seeing Gerry locked away or hearing the snide remarks when she went to the shops or even to the church. At no stage did she ever delude herself with thoughts of Gerry's recovery. The hospital was seen as serving three functions in the community: detention, retribution and deterrence. It kept people who were judged to be dangerous out of circulation, it punished those who transgressed conventional mores and it kept people from straying off the narrow path, otherwise they might face a fate worse than jail, incarceration in 'the madhouse'. Nobody really believed that anybody went there to be healed.

Every time relatives went to visit loved ones in the hospital they shivered. Perhaps the most chilling part of the unpleasant ordeal was the sound of the rustling of keys as the 'inmates' were locked in their cells. The keys were symbols of power and authority for the nurses, and for the patients they were a constant reminder of their subservience.

When a wife saw her husband for that first time she could have shed a million tears. His featureless, grey cell would induce nothing only despair and was so tiny as to guarantee feelings of claustrophobia for someone who was used to an active life.

The process of institutionalisation was itself a form of psychological internment, a malignant force which stripped people of their humanity and left them incapable of independent thought. The primary objective was docility; the 'inmates' were no longer a menace to society. Like condemned prisoners serving out their sentence, they were compelled to bathe communally, just another humiliation in a long catalogue of degradation. Many would have been happy just to be in a place with no other voices, no other clutter, but with space for relaxing and thinking. They must have pined for a little time in the day that was really their own: a little escape which would refresh and rejuvenate them. The erosion of personal dignity and privacy, the dead emotions and listless eyes were unavoidable side-effects required to keep the system flowing smoothly. Nobody seemed to question or even notice the perversion in the situation where the system became more important than the people it was designed to serve.

Time passed slowly in the cells. It was like a human zoo, without the visitors. There was nothing to do but waste away. At first relatives wondered why no one ever made a speech about mental hospitals in Dáil Eireann or talked about it on television. There were no votes in the mentally ill. They were just 'the shadows of the human race'.

Although families brought the courage of lions to their struggles with their loved one's disability, they were not able to readily cope with mental illness. People could not even bring themselves to use the words 'mental illness', but the odium was obvious even when the comments were relatively mild. In rural Ireland in particular, appearance and reality seldom coincided. Although on the surface there was an egalitarian community animated by the altruistic ideals of Christianity, the reality was that a sophisticated, subtle caste system was in operation. At the very bottom of the human scrapheap were those who suffered from mental illness. Just one step up were their families, with members of the travelling community at more or less the same level.

Down through the years I have known many Elizabeths and Gerrys and, because of my own trials, I can readily share their pain.

## The Heart Is a Lonely Hunter
While lack of money and facilities are huge problems for the disabled, I am particularly concerned about their emotional deprivation. I shudder for those experiencing intense isolation in the encircling

darkness of their lives in an institution where they feel they are just bed numbers. In my periods of hospitalisation I did not sparkle the way I normally did. There were glimpses of my real self, but the old magic was gone. I was serious, even sullen. Looking back, with the benefit of hindsight, I can see now that I was on the brink of clinical depression. It was as if I had been trapped in endless days of blackness. The hours passed slowly, tunnels with no light and no end. I was unable to relate normally to family and friends. Even the simplest task became a mountain for me to climb. Each new day was a fresh agony of fear. I was unable to ask for help, though sometimes Jimmy's cheery words could lift the veil that enveloped me for a while.

Loneliness was a crowded hospital room for me. When I sought help from those around me, they said nothing. I would have preferred it if they had been angry. I just could not handle the silence. Something inside me snapped. I felt so isolated and had, literally, nowhere to go for help when Jimmy was not around. I often found myself near to tears but in my heart there was something stirring, a sense of outrage, a feeling of total despair. I hoped fervently that my soul would be set free from its anguish and that I would find peace at last in a higher, more perfect world.

I saw my disability as God's test of my faith. I compared my fate to that of the Bible story of Abraham being asked to sacrifice his son.

A determined campaigner on disability issues, I am willing to fight to the bitter end. My formal schooling was skimpy, but I have accumulated a wide range of knowledge and skills not designated by the Department of Education's curriculum. Although I left school at fourteen, my real education began when MS struck me down, that's where the lessons were about life and the knocks hard. I want to ensure that disabled people have all the support they need and I want to provide them with a gilt-edged opportunity to unlock some of their potential.

More than anything else, I want disabled people to be seen for what they are: people with a heart larger than the world in which they live – a world which is not ready to understand them properly and cannot see the beauty in them. In spite of all the humiliation they have so bravely endured, with such resilience and such dignity, the most persuasive of all images of the disabled remains people unbroken in body and spirit alike.

In 2003, to mark the European Year of People with Disabilities and the Special Olympics, the Catholic Church published *Life in all its fullness*, a letter from the Irish Catholic Bishops' Conference.

The document recognises that while progress has been made in some areas much more remains to be done if people with disabilities are to play their full part in the life of the Church. To quote: 'Most parishes have made efforts to make their buildings more accessible and user-friendly, for example, through the provision of loop systems, the improvement of lighting and the installation of ramps. We must reflect on the importance of making the liturgy more accessible to people with learning disabilities. In general, we need a greater consciousness of how everyone can be made welcome in our community, our rituals and our celebrations.'

Taking as its inspiration the words from John's Gospel – 'I have come in order that you might have life – life in all its fullness' – the letter is full of thought-provoking comments. However, what is most striking is the way it avoids pious platitudes and confronts difficult questions. 'This European Year of People with Disabilities was an opportune time to invite people with disabilities to give their views on how best they may become involved in all aspects of Church life and ministry. Do our prejudices restrict us in recognising the giftedness of people with disabilities and the richness that their participation would bring to Church life?'

It goes on to ask a series of specific questions. For example: Are parish councils and committees representative of all? Are children and young people with disabilities welcomed and encouraged to participate in parish youth clubs and groups?

In addition, the pastoral letter floats a number of practical suggestions that the Church might consider at local level to bring the disabled in from the margins. It suggests: 'Perhaps supportive networks could be developed at diocesan level to empower each local parish to be more inclusive of all.' More practically, it asks if church and parish information could be made available in as many different formats as possible such as Braille, large print and audio.

## Enemies of the State

Since my cure I have acquired a huge admiration for Kathy Sinnott and the long and difficult campaign she fought to get rights for her autistic son Jamie; in the process highlighting that children with intellectual disabilities deserve an appropriate education. She was convinced that Ireland treated children like Jamie as 'enemies of the state' because they required significant resources and, as a result, the state fought tooth and nail not to give them their rights.

Kathy began to seriously reflect on the role of the family in equalising opportunity after she had just received a successful High Court judgement which had named and shamed the Irish State for inequality of treatment not just of her son Jamie and others like him but of herself and of her family. Justice Barr's wise judgement rightly acknowledged the rights and shared welfare of the disabled and their families.

The case highlights three requirements for social change.

1. A change in the way in which we think about disability.
2. A removal of the many barriers which prevent people with learning disabilities from using ordinary services and participating in everyday activities.
3. A need to discover what kinds of support are needed to ensure that anyone with a learning disability really does have the same opportunities as their non-disabled neighbour.

The Irish Constitution says that 'all citizens shall, as human persons be held equal'.

The answer has to be: don't put limitations on people, but find opportunities. For example, when I meet people who are blind, they say to me, 'Don't tell me I can't do the job show me how to do it.' Blindness isn't the problem. It is the prejudices and short-sightedness of sighted people that cause the problems.

One story shows this clearly. Some blind and visually impaired young women were being forced to travel to Northern Ireland for their education, owing to the lack of facilities in the Republic. One case I know of was that of a fifteen-year-old girl from the west of Ireland who spent her weekdays as a student in Belfast and was fostered on weekends because it was impossible for her to travel home every weekend. I find it incomprehensible that in this day and age such a situation is allowed to develop.

To take another example, there are many people who are literally living lives of quiet desperation because of a stammer. I know there are people out there whose lives have been shattered because they didn't get the help they needed. One of the saddest parts of my life is when I get heart-rending letters from people who have stammers and who, because of that, are unable to make social connections. Some people in this situation can have very few friends.

I think part of the problem is that for too long the focus, when it came to people with disabilities, was on charity. One of the big advances that has finally happened is that people now see disability issues as questions of justice and rights.

I found no villains anywhere. On the contrary, one could not be but impressed by the hard work and dedication of those in charge of the services. But how could so many honourable people, who were undoubtedly charitable and competent, allow so many terrible situations to develop?

The awful thing is that there are people who are going through now what I went through thirty-five years ago. All around Ireland there are parents with disabled children who are asking two questions: 'How can I get a proper education for my child with disabilities?' and 'What will happen to my child when I die?'

I will not accept excuses. I will be a voice for those people who are too tired, disabled or incapacitated to stake their rightful claim to better services in Ireland. I will be a voice for those who might not have noticed that the Celtic Tiger ever existed. I will be a voice which will clearly state that those people who depend on our educational services will no longer be treated as second-class citizens. I will be a voice which will never allow hard-nosed politicians to forget their responsibilities to all the citizens of Ireland, not just the wealthy elite.

The longer I live, the more I realise the impact attitude can have on people's lives. We cannot change our past. We cannot change the inevitable. The only thing we can do is play on the one string we have – namely our attitude. It is said that life is ten per cent what happens to you and ninety per cent how you react to it. When you cannot change the direction of the wind, adjust your sails. I do not judge those who try and fail, but only those who fail to try.

What matters in this life is more than winning for ourselves: what matters is helping others win, even if it means slowing down and changing our course.

Some years ago, at the Seattle Special Olympics, nine disabled contestants assembled at the starting line for the hundred-yard dash. At the gun, they all took off in haste. Things were going according to plan until one little boy stumbled on the track, fell, and started to cry. The other eight heard the boy cry. They slowed down and looked back. They all turned around and went back, every one of them. One girl with Down Syndrome bent down and kissed the fallen boy and said, 'This will make it better.'

Then all nine linked arms and walked together to the finish line. Everyone in the stadium stood and cheered.

Each of us must begin to accept responsibility for the society we now live in – the one we have created and the one that we all sustain. We have developed a great capacity to exonerate ourselves from our personal responsibilities by creating a blame culture. We blame others for the shortcomings of our society while we demand more and more for ourselves. It is time to stop whinging about the deficiencies of our society and accept responsibility – after all, we get the society we deserve. Justice is totally dependent on us human beings.

The quality of the life of a community is measured by the care given to the weakest, especially the sick and disabled. We must begin by putting human needs and values at the very top of our priority list – 'people first' must be our new motto. We must involve people of all ages in deciding their futures by putting in place at local and national level adequate consultative structures to ensure that people from every sector of our society have an opportunity to have their say and to be heard. We must actively promote and enshrine in our everyday lives human values based on respect, human rights, equal opportunities, compassion, justice and forgiveness. These values must become the very foundation of our future society. All policy issues and developments must be tested and measured against these principles.

One of John B. Keane's creations, Dan Paddy Andy O'Sullivan, famously said, 'You'll never have peace in this country until every man has more than the next.' We appear to have reached that stage. While the strong prevail, the weak are thrown out to the side. We are so conditioned to reward the strong and penalise the weak that we do not take the time to ask why was that person weak in the first place. In recent years, no other question has dominated my thinking like that one.

## Champion of the Disabled

Since the death of Pope John Paul II in 2005, there has been much discussion about his legacy. Understandably, there has been much of this discussion has focused on his rich social teaching, his ecumenical concerns and his work for peace. One area, though, that has not got the attention it deserved was Pope John Paul II's attitude to disability.

'The quality of life of a community is measured by the care given to the weakest, especially the disabled.' These were the words of Pope John Paul II.

In the course of a lengthy message, the late Holy Father began by outlining the Christian view of the situation:

'The disabled person, even when wounded in the mind or in his sensorial and intellective capacities, is a fully human individual, with the sacred and inalienable rights proper to every creature. The human being, in fact, regardless of the conditions in which he lives his life and the capacities that he might manifest, possesses a unique dignity and singular value starting from the beginning of his existence until the moment of natural death. The person of the disabled, with all his limitations and sufferings, compels us to question ourselves with respect and wisdom on the mystery of man. The more we penetrate the dark and unknown areas of human reality, the more we understand that precisely in the most difficult and disquieting situations the dignity and grandeur of the human beings.'

John Paul II went on to point out that the wounded humanity of the disabled challenges us to acknowledge, accept and promote in each one of these sisters and brothers of ours the incomparable value of the human being created by God. He went on to make a call for practical measures that many campaigners for the disabled in Ireland would strongly agree with:

> 'There is a subtle form of discrimination in the policies and educational projects that try to hide or deny the deficiencies of the disabled person, proposing styles of life and objectives that do not correspond to their reality and in the end are frustrating and unjust. The recognition of rights must be followed, therefore, by the sincere commitment of all to create concrete conditions of life, support structures and juridical guarantees capable of responding to the needs and the dynamics of growth of the disabled person and those who share his situation, beginning with his relatives. People with mental handicap perhaps have greater need of care, affection, understanding and love. They cannot be left alone, defenceless or unprotected, in the difficult task of facing life.'

People with disabilities allow us the opportunity to share the wisdom of people whom God has seemingly made so different, a vision of God which we might not perceive in other people. This is part of the biblical tradition:

'Though this outer man may be falling into decay, the inner man is renewed day by day. Yes the troubles which are soon over, though they weigh little, train us for the carrying of a weight of eternal glory which is out of all proportion to them. And so we have no eyes for the things that are visible, but only for things that are invisible; for visible things last only for a time, and the invisible things are eternal.'

In making these comments, the late Pope performed an invaluable prophetic service for our world today. His exhortation reminds us that when it comes to rights for the disabled it is a case of a lot done – a lot more to do. It is right and fitting that the Church should be at the heart of this campaign, as from the outset Jesus publicly aligned himself with the poor and the outcasts. The Church which Jesus called for was therefore a radical presence, which empowered all people to have a meaningful life.

Particular concern must be taken with children with disabilities. In the family, which is a community of persons, special attention must be devoted to the children by developing a profound esteem for their personal dignity, and a great respect and a generous concern for their rights. This is true for every child, but it comes all the more urgent the smaller the child is and the more she or he is need of everything, when she or he is sick, suffering or disabled.

## *Getting Our Act Together*

My own experience of illness and disability have made me very aware of the need for practical measures to care for those who are unable to care for themselves. I strongly believe that the quality of life of a community is measured by the care given to the weakest, especially the sick and disabled. The wounded humanity of the disabled and seriously ill challenges us all to acknowledge, accept and promote in each one of these sisters and brothers of ours the incomparable value of the human being created by God.

Like many campaigners for the disabled in Ireland, I am adamant that the world of rights cannot be the prerogative of the able-bodied. The participation in the life of society of each and every disabled person must be facilitated, to whatever degree possible. All must be enabled to develop all their potential. A society that only makes room for those who it deem to be 'fully functional', completely autonomous and independent, is not a society worthy of the human being. Discrimination in virtue of efficiency is no less to be frowned upon than that in virtue of race or gender or religion. I believe that the recognition of rights must be followed, therefore, by the sincere commitment of all to create concrete conditions of life, support structures and juridical guarantees capable of responding to the needs and the dynamics of growth of the disabled person and those who share their situation, beginning with their relatives and carers. People with severe illnesses or disabilities cannot be left alone, defenceless or unprotected, in the difficult task of facing life. Apart from bringing the Good News to people, I want to do my bit to ensure that those who are struggling have their voices heard.

I am anchored by my encounter with God's presence dwelling within people with disabilities and by a shared commitment to the philosophy of Pope Francis in Croke Park during his visit to Ireland in 2018:

> 'The Church is the family of God's children. A family in which we rejoice with those who are rejoicing, and weep with those who grieve or feel knocked down by life. A family in which we care for everyone, for God our Father has made all of us his children in Baptism.'

*Imagine all the People*

There is a story that tells of how, one evening when Pope John XXIII was having dinner, his secretary came in and reported with disdain dripping out of his mouth that a particular priest had been involved in a minor misdeed which would cause embarrassment to the Church.

The Pope took the secretary by surprise when he pointed to the beautiful wine glass he was drinking out of and said: 'Who does this belong to?'

The secretary said incredulously: 'To you, your Eminence.'

Then Pope John XXIII took up the glass and smashed it to smithereens on the floor and asked: 'Now who does to belong to?'

'It's still yours your Eminence.'

It was a very dramatic illustration of the fact that the Church is for the bruised, battered and the broken.

Hope is a passion for what is possible. My hope and my passion is for a better deal for the disabled.

Some people think there is no prejudice. I say to them: Look harder.

If one person suffers we all do.

If one person falls we all fall.

Imagine a world where everyone was treated fairly.

Imagine a world where nobody feels left behind.

Imagine a country where nobody feels unwanted.

Let us not just imagine – let us try harder to do better.

We can do better.

We must do better.

# 11

# A New Role

*'All which I took from thee I did but take*
*not for thy harms,*
*But just that thou might'st seek it in My arms.'*

— FRANCIS THOMPSON, 'The Hound of Heaven'

The atmosphere is electric, like a revivalist meeting with a touch of fanaticism. The crowd wait for me to come up to the podium like a presidential candidate. As I speak, all eyes are on me, seemingly transfixed. It appears that if I had asked the crowd to try walking on water they would have been happy to do so. At least that is what always happens in my dreams!

Initially I was flattered, honoured but absolutely petrified when asked to speak in public. But, as they say: *Ní threabhadh tú pairc go brách á chasadh timpeall i do intinn* ('You'll never plough a field by turning it over in your mind.') As letting the 'cause' down was anathema to me, I went on stage that day in 1990, despite my shaking hands and wobbly knees.

There was just a slight tremor in my voice as I intoned my opening words. Public speaking was something I never dreamed of.

It is said that courage is not the absence of fear, but rather the judgement that something else is more important than fear. If we turn away from a challenge once, it is so much easier to do the same again the next time, and the next. Showing some courage in less serious difficulties is often the best training for the major crises. Courage is like a muscle. It is strengthened with use. I have found it easier to speak in public with experience.

It has taken a long time to get to this stage.

Nowadays, the first impression you might have of my home just outside Athlone is of a bizarre combination of train station and radio chat show – with its incessant movement of people and a phone that is perpetually ringing. The rest of the family transmit welcome like electricity. They are like young children on Christmas morning. The enthusiasm of visitors both contributes to and feeds off their delight. It is a virtuous circle of joy.

A man calls with a sick young child cradled in his arms, another witness in the court of human suffering. He is looking for a blessing and longing for words of consolation, hoping against hope that his daughter will get a miracle cure from healing hands. On the table are six letters. The postmarks read Waterford, Tyrone, Canada, England, Australia and Castlerea. Another six to add to the hundreds of letters from people who have been touched by my story.

The irony of all of this is that I am a most unlikely and unwilling candidate for celebrity status on a grand scale; I am not the kind of woman to have my head easily turned by adulation. I try to exude a decency and a warmth that is not always available to people who never seem to have a moment to call their own. I have no time for pretensions or arrogance.

People tell me that my sentences provide an invaluable insight into my mind and character, as apparently I seem to have difficulty constructing a sentence without reference to God or one of the Holy Family. When I speak I have the struggle of someone trying to come to terms with their own limitations. Talking to me, people are spared facile answers, pious platitudes or cheap slogans. Instead I hope people are confronted by a woman with a rocklike faith. But, despite my strong faith, I am not cocooned from the reality of the world around me.

Although thoughts of godliness are as natural to me as breathing, I have not been seduced into ignoring the problems which people have today. In fact, I nurture a deep desire to see a more loving and just society created. As a mother of two adults, I have a particular concern for the plight of young people in today's world.

Inevitably, when I think of young people, my attention turns to my children. A new range of emotions comes to the fore as I remember their early years. The great regret of my life is that my physical condition prevented me from being the type of mother that I wished to be. This sense of regret has never been erased as befits a woman who has experienced an enormous personal loss. The passion and sheer excitement of talking about the Holy Family is totally dissipated, and when I think back on that time my eyes moisten. It is evident that I still feel a pronounced sense of personal trauma. The normal flow of my speech is impaired. Pauses appear between sentences. My voice drops to a whisper.

I try to express myself simply and in a way that everyone can understand. My messages are universal – faith, family, trust, love, surrender, goodness – but when I am giving talks in a church hall I try and prevent them from becoming abstractions and instead give them a real flesh and blood quality and original beauty. I can empathise with loneliness and despair, with a sense of crisis and being in the abyss. I know the struggle between darkness and faith, between passion and hope, and between the real and the counterfeit.

Everything about my dealings with my family is full of warmth and conviction. When I am invited to speak I try to unmask fear and proclaim the triumph of love and the victory of a healing God.

In my strength and simplicity I touch on the core of the human spirit, where the whole fragile world of women and men meets – as a woman who found strength in weakness and victory in defeat. My power is not in what I preach, but in what I have come through to live. My illness helped me to find the secret of transforming my life with meaning and, in doing so, I hope to become a source of light and life for others as well.

## Searching for a New Role

In the first few months after my cure, I kept asking myself: why me, why was I chosen to be cured? The answer came while saying the Family Rosary six months later. That gift was not to me alone, but to the people of the world, to let them know that God was there, and that all people had to do was to ask and they would receive. People tell me prayer has not worked for them, but just as we are very good at telling our children what is best for them, God knows what is best for us.

A few months after my cure I said to Jimmy that the family would go to Medjugorje, before the year was out. He just laughed out loud and asked: 'On what. Fresh air or hot water?' Although we could not afford to even think about it, somebody paid anonymously for us to go there. We were thrilled! But during Mass there, I had a very unusual experience. My hands seemed to have a life of their own and were opening out wide. Around each hand there was a beautiful glow of light. I feared I was hallucinating.

## Revelation

The glow was the glow of love. It looked like there was a single heart in the palm of each of my hands. They stayed like that for the rest of

Mass. It was as if my hands were in the Lord's hands. There was just one pulse – the pulse that is the love in his heart for people. I turned to Our Lady's altar and said the Hail Mary.

After Mass I had a desire to go to confession and the priest said to me: 'Would you lay your hands on me and pray with me? You have been given a very special gift from God.' All I could say was: 'May the Lord help me, because I knew nothing about this.' During that whole trip my cup of happiness was overflowing, although it took me a year to figure out all that happened. I know now that God was telling me that my cure was not for myself, but so that I could go and spread the news of God's love and healing to others.

Having returned home from my trip I went to my bishop and asked him for permission to speak from the altar at my local church. I now give healing ministries at various churches throughout Ireland. I anoint people on the forehead with an oil I call the 'oil of gladness'. I then lay my hands on them and pray with them. People have claimed to have been healed physically, mentally and spiritually at my healing ministries. I am very acutely aware of the fact that if I am to help bring God to others I must remain in close touch with God myself.

*Behind Every Great Woman . . .*
With practical Jimmy at my side, telling me not to be daft when he thought it was right and laughing at me now and again with a smile in his eye when I was losing the run of myself, I move ahead. Few men complement a woman as does Jimmy complement me. He has helped me through many a bad patch and there were times I felt he could read my mind. Any time I am in a tizzy, I turn to Jimmy and the practical side to him, the provider and husband – the essential

goodness you get in a decent man – sorts out any problems for me with basic common sense. Even to the extent that Jimmy generally drove me everywhere, as I never learned to drive. As is said in the west of Ireland, Jimmy has 'no side to him' – no hidden agenda. He just wants to be a good father and husband.

He makes light of the inconveniences which my new ministry imposes on him. This is a time for rejoicing. During the long course of my illness Jimmy had kept up a brave face, but his eyes alone failed to hide the grievous, awful sense of desperation and impending loss. He has seen his wife transformed from a broken wreck to a what he tells me is a confident public speaker and, I hope, an impressive communicator – as at home speaking to a small group in the local church to a rigorous interview on national television.

In Jimmy's case, familiarity with my story certainly does not breed contempt. When someone asked him about this, he told them, 'I have sat and listened to Marion's story over and over again. I never get tired of hearing it and I can't get over the miracle of seeing her standing there at the altar so full of life and health, after what she has been through.'

Once I asked Jimmy to evaluate me as a speaker and this what he told me:

'Watching you speak to a packed gathering is an arresting experience. Little flames flicker from the half-dozen lighted candles – symbols of peace, goodness and hope. People have come from miles around. The congregation is riveted. Rarely in living memory has a sermon being so attentively listened to in this church. The audience had often been given more scholarly and elegant sermons, but the public baring of your soul was much more powerful. When you had stopped talking, the crowd pause again, this time for some to wipe the tears from their eyes. Afterwards, scores of people line up in the sacristy to meet this ordinary woman, to shake her hand and to draw solace and inspiration from her extraordinary story.

'You have an aura about you. You radiate enthusiasm and even when you have grounds for complaint you are always positive. Even more importantly you inspire these qualities in those around you. People feel good about themselves when you are around them.'

## Good God

As someone who has spent a lifetime studying, in various ways, words, I can't help but admire the statement in the Gospel: 'In the beginning was the Word and the Word was with God and the Word was with God.'

One of the things that also really interests me is the nature of goodness. I am fascinated by Christianity and the figure of Christ. I constantly marvel at the fact that those who are followers of Christianity believe that even before we were born and long after we die, there is at work a provident, gracious God who has created us and loves us and wants us to share in God's own life. This view shapes the Christian's moral life by enabling them to live in faith, in hope and in love. Accordingly, Christianity issues us with an invitation into the heart of what it is to be human. I love the idea of the divinisation being most tellingly revealed by our humanisation.

I love the idea of a religion that is based on love. This is best summed up in the quotation from St Paul: 'To live through love in God's presence.' Every day I open the papers and I read stories about the absence of love in the world and it depresses me.

Love of God is expressed not only in prayer and Sunday worship, but must permeate every aspect of our lives. The Bible has no ambiguities on one issue: you cannot love God unless you love your neighbour.

The Old Testament prophets were scathing in their criticism of those who sought to appease God by prayers and sacrifices while oppressing the powerless. Jesus told us that all the law and the prophets are summarised in the commandment to love God and the neighbour. No words are minced when we are told: 'Whoever claims to love God but hates his brother or sister is a liar.' All love invites love. God calls us to love.

I am enthralled by the compassion of God and of Jesus. There are days when I'm very far away from this, but I'm always inspired by the image of Jesus in the Gospels. He was someone who brought the compassion of God to people, someone who didn't judge or condemn. He was someone who was with people wherever they were, especially those who found themselves on the margins of society. That is why I really admire people like Sr Stanislaus Kennedy and Fr Peter McVerry because of the work they do with people who are unable to help themselves.

I believe very much that your father and mother and your family and your background are very important. Christianity can be inherited as a faith and may not appear in any obvious form, but in subtle forms, like in notions of love and fair play.

Prayer is an important component in my life. The recognition of the importance of prayer is particularly relevant to today. 'That's only a contemplative order' is a phrase one sometimes hears when people are talking about religious life. Apart from what it betrays about our understanding of religious life, it also says something about our attitude to prayer. It is as if prayer is on the periphery of the Christian life, instead of at the very centre. In the hustle and bustle of our everyday lives, it is often difficult to find the inner stillness to make space for God to speak to us. Much of prayer is the struggle to overcome our many distractions, to concentrate on the presence of God. Solitude is a fertile state of mind and spirit in which it is possible to concentrate on something for a long time and also to establish a relationship with whatever you are concentrating on. I know the importance of spending time alone with God.

I have particular affection for the Hail Mary and Rosary, as I have for the Mass, but I wonder if we take the idea of the church as the house of God seriously enough. It is crucially important that everyone is made to feel welcome.

Christianity illuminates my personal and 'professional' life, notably in my preaching style. Christ's capacity to extract a positive message from the darkest situation is a source of enduring fascination for me. I try to emulate this aspect of Christ's personality when I interact with people. Again, in emulation of Christ, my aim is always to be constructive. I would be very concerned if I ever offended anybody or caused any pain.

## Public Property

Humility is a great virtue in Athlone! My neighbours are pretty decent when it comes to my 'fame' and don't ever bother me. I think the trick is if you present an air of being inaccessible you can create problems for yourself, but if you don't have airs and graces people will let you be.

One friend has taught me the lesson of humility well. I will always remember the first time my father came to see me speak in public. We were in the kitchen afterwards and she said, 'God, I suppose it was all right. It was fairly good and you were fairly good.' This was high praise indeed!

I laugh at the memory of two old ladies who came to visit me one day, who were not as highly impressed as others. One had a bad back and the other a bad foot. I blessed them and prayed with them.

When they were leaving they asked how much they owed me. I said, 'Nothing but a prayer.' As they were going out to the car I heard one of them saying to the other, 'She can't be much good she didn't charge us.' You just can't win!

Bitter experience has taught me that if someone wants to find fault with you they will. It is a bit like the story of the Garda sergeant, a total so-and-so, who was on his last day in the town before he retired from the force. He was a mean and spiteful man and had 'caught' everyone in the town for some offence or other. The only person who had escaped was the parish priest. The garda was determined to rectify that situation on his last day. He knew that the priest always cycled home after saying morning Mass, so the garda stood at the bottom of the hill. His plan had been to step out in front of the priest, forcing him to swerve and topple over and then he could 'do him' for dangerous driving. He carried out his plan, but although the priest swerved he kept control of his bike. The priest stopped to wish the garda well on his retirement. The cop said, 'Jesus, you were fierce lucky not to fall then.'

The priest replied, 'Indeed I was lucky but then I had God with me.'

The garda nearly danced for joy as he said, 'I'm doing you for having two on a bike.'

### Foster & Allen

Little things can mean a lot. At the height of my illness one night, Jimmy brought me to a hotel for a meal. He had to go to the toilet and Tony Allen, one half of the famous duo Foster & Allen, who was in the hotel at the time, came over to keep me company. It was a very kind gesture and one I appreciated very much. Now I try to do all I can to help people in need.

My frequent travels have led many to assume that I am making a small fortune in my ministry. The reality is the opposite. I am philosophical about this begrudgery. When people are talking about us someone else is left alone.

I ask the same questions, wrestle with the same problems and face the same pain and anguish as anyone in my audience. I too have confronted the loneliness and despair that so many people suffer from in Ireland today. My faith and love have not shielded me from pain and anguish. I persevered in my struggle and through the sheer force of my love and my burning desire to know the true heart of God, I discovered for myself and for others the core truths of Christianity. I can relate to people well because I express myself simply and in a way everyone can understand. Everything about my sharing is full of life and conviction and I try to impress my own 'stamp' on a fresh and original expression of the Christian message. My aim is to be an inspiring shortcut to the Gospel message.

My message sometimes echoes that of St John of Cross:

'Where there is no love, put love, and you will find love . . . in the evening of our lives we will be judged on our love.'

Although the word 'love' is often misused and misrepresented for personal greed, there is a tremendous outpouring of love all about us. This is evident in the tears of sympathy and compassion, in the many heroic lives of the carers for the sick and the downtrodden. It shines forth in the bond that unites families and communities, in millions of tiny acts of goodness and kindness that are performed every day.

In 'Easter, 1916', W.B. Yeats wrote:

> *'Too long a sacrifice*
> *Can make a stone of the heart.'*

Many who write to me are victims because of abuse, unwanted pregnancies, broken marriages, shattered relationships. Brokenness is the rule rather than the exception. Some are coming to terms with the fact that they have created a situation that is irrevocable; something that can never be the same again – crippled by the circumstances and mistakes of their past, they go through life with an air of hopelessness. For some, the wound has healed but the scar remains.

Many people who come to me are lonely, and in need of companionship and love. I believe that the greatest gift I can give to another is the gift of my time – time to listen, time to care, time to make them feel worthwhile. One can do a lot of good if you don't want to take credit for it.

Sartre famously said: 'Hell is other people.' Heaven also is other people and the Other who is love. God has given me so much that I want to do something in return. The Lord has blessed me with a ministry to families. I tour Ireland, England and Scotland at the invitation of local priests hoping to help the sick. I only go where I'm invited by the priest to give a healing ministry. The Lord has blessed me greatly, but I personally have no healing power. I cannot heal. No one can heal, only Jesus.

It came as a great tribute when I was invited by Sr Briege McKenna to speak at a special conference for priests at All Hallows. A treasured souvenir in my family home is a framed photograph of me blessing the throat of singer John MacNally when I bumped into him as we were both visiting friends and relatives in a nursing home.

My aim is to show people what Christian love is in the concrete situation. I was not afraid of dying after my cure, but there was this question inside me: 'What have I done for others?' I knew I hadn't done much to hurt them, but also I know that I hadn't done as much to help them as I wish.

President Dwight D. Eisenhower once said:

> 'Every gun that is made, every warship launched, every rocket fired, signifies a theft from those who hunger and are not fed, those who are cold and have not clothes. The world in arms is not spending money alone. It's spending the sweat of its labourers, the genius of scientists and the hopes of its children.'

I have never said fine words like that, but I feel I do not need to because it was by my actions that I spoke louder and more effectively.

I want to serve. I can be a bridge between those who have and those who have less.

My main flashpoint is not the number of problems, nor the scale of the problems, but our collective failure to do anything to solve them. When action is called for, too often we respond simply with platitudes. When confronted with problems, we simply wash our hands à la Pontius Pilate. My frustration is not with our actions, but with our non-actions, by our collective sins of omission. If we are not part of the solution we are part of the problem. I believed that we are too inclined to put the difficult thing on the back burner. Instead we should do the difficult thing as soon as possible because that way there is instant relief.

Today there are three possible responses for us to follow. We might be prophets announcing the better age to come. Alternatively we could be preservers making sure that in the flux of life the validity of past insights will not be lost. However, I chose a third approach: to share the drama of the age and work for the advancement of society and of the common good.

*Our Friends in the North*
I have made a number of trips to Northern Ireland and I am very aware of the legacy of the violence.

The Troubles have produced many unforgettable moments like that of the late Gordon Wilson offering words of forgiveness in Enniskillen after the massacre on Remembrance Sunday that killed his daughter, Marie, in 1987. Immediately after the carnage caused by an IRA bomb, communal passions threatened to explode. In this highly charged atmosphere Gordon Wilson's words of forgiveness diffused an extremely volatile situation. Even the hardest heart could not but have been melted by his intensely moving account of how he lay bleeding under the rubble, clutching his daughter's hand and heard her fading voice saying, 'Daddy, I love you very much.'

Another of the defining images of the Troubles will always be that of Fr Edward Daly, on Bloody Sunday, waving a white bloodstained handkerchief, as he led a group of men carrying the limp body of a teenager away from the hail of bullets and ever mounting bloodbath. That day in 1972 was one of the watershed moments in Anglo–Irish history. The anger of all Nationalist Ireland was reflected in the torching of the British Embassy in Dublin. Bloody Sunday seemed to touch a deep nerve with everybody. It brought to the surface a wellspring of latent anti-English feeling, with all sorts of grievances, real and imagined, about English involvement in Irish history. The burning of the British Embassy in Dublin starkly illustrated the ambivalent attitude which many Irish people had to political violence.

People in Northern Ireland on both sides paid the price of the political conflict in a more emotionally engaging and humanising way. There were almost modern incarnations of the Romeo and Juliet story in the plight of the girls who were tarred and feathered because they had the temerity to love a boy from 'the wrong side'.

I cannot change history. I cannot solve the political problems. But, in my small way, when I go to Northern Ireland I can bring a bit of comfort to people who have suffered a lot. As I know from my own personal experience, a little bit of comfort is important when you feel your world is caving in.

## Listen and Learn

After one of the talks I gave, I was asked to define happiness. I said I was not able to do so myself, but I offered the Chinese understanding of happiness. In their analysis of happiness, they decided that it is broken into three elements. The first is to have something in life to work for. The second is to have something in life to dream for. The third is to have someone to love. I have been lucky on each of these three fronts, but I have to work at it.

There is a limit to the amount of resolution you can muster from your own resources. I am fortunate in having plenty of support to draw on. When things hit rock bottom, you need the example and inspiration of others to help sustain your will to fight the good fight. I have learned so much from being a wife and parent. Probably the biggest lesson I have learned is that we need to rest our tongues and use our ears. We speak too much in haste. We cut each other to the quick in temper and we can never take back the spoken word. When a child makes a mistake or does wrong, they do not need to hear about it every day. We all know when we have overstepped our brief and the last thing we need is to be reminded: 'I've told you time and time again.' This is harmful talk. It hurts deeply. The scars remain for life. We need to give breathing space in moments of anger. What is not said today can always be said tomorrow.

The most fundamental thing is to be loved, to be accepted as I am, warts and all. The best way to do that is to be quiet and listen to other people. That is the toughest discipline of all the disciplines. To listen may be almost the greatest service any human being performs for another.

There is no substitute for kindness. Acts of kindness are contagious, just like germs – only kindness does not make you sick, but the very opposite. If kindness does not work for another human being, nothing else will.

My ministry leaves me in full agreement with Hilaire Belloc's lines in 'Courtesy':

*'Yet in my walks it seems to me*
*That the Grace of God is in courtesy.'*

Such acts of kindness must not be seen only in materialistic terms. Some of the most profound kindness will centre around words, empathy, understanding, being non-judgemental, recognising the person as an equal human being, expressing positive and encouraging comments and sometimes and, very importantly, just being with the person, however broken they might be. Indeed, spending time with a vulnerable person is the most valuable support of all. How much does a friendly face cost? Nothing.

*Selected Correspondence*
I receive a massive mail bag from those seeking my help and intercession, and from those who have been helped. A few letters sent to me gives a flavour of my ministry.

*Dear Marion,*

*I wish to confirm that since I last saw you my health has dramatically improved. As you know I have had Lupus Nephritis of the kidneys for over ten years now. It is a disease of the Immune system which attacks the kidneys and can cause damage. I was told on my last visit to hospital that I might even get eventual kidney failure. I am on steroids every day and also blood pressure tablets. My blood pressure goes up because of the disease and also because of the steroids. Indeed last year I collapsed because an ulcer burst in my stomach and I lost between five and six pints of blood due to steroids attacking the lining of my stomach. I have to take two tablets per day to help heal it. That was a year ago and I still had pain up until I saw you and could only eat certain types of food.*

*After my last visit to you I got an urge not to take my stomach tablet. I must point out that many times before this I forgot to take my tablet but was soon reminded by the sharp pain and indigestion I would get. However, I decided to give it a try and not only do I not need the tablet anymore but I can eat what I like and have never had an ache or pain in my stomach since. I would truly say this is a miracle as you can gather I have been tortured for many years now.*

*As well as my stomach being cured I have a feeling that some-thing also has happened regarding my kidneys. They started all of a sudden since my visit to you to function much better and I feel and look much healthier.*

*God bless you.*

*C.*

*Dear Marion*

*After the healing Mass, at Saints Peter and Paul Church, on Thursday 11th November 1993, I brought my daughter Sarah to you, and asked you to give her a special blessing, as she had to have an operation the following Tuesday. That operation was to remove a growth, from under her arm, which was caused by 'rapid cell division' – or in other words cancer!*

*All my prayers were answered. When they operated, they found no cancer. All they had to remove was a 'growth'. The surgeons and staff at the hospital were both surprised, and extremely delighted. Although beforehand they could not say 100% it was cancer, that is what they had expected to find, and had prepared us for this.*

*I am convinced that through you, God performed a miracle at that Mass, and cured Sarah (even her recovery from the operation has amazed doctors). I thank God daily for us, but would also like to thank you, from the bottom of my heart. I cannot tell you how listening to you at that Mass helped me. I feel my and my family's faith is stronger now, and all I can say is: 'Keep up the good work.'*

*Thank you very much.*

*Ch.*

*Dear Marion,*

*Just a note to say that I had a beautiful girl on August 12th. She came four weeks early, wasn't due until September, but is thriving very well. I just want to say thank you most sincerely, I never forget you in my prayers, and wouldn't have her today only for your wonderful prayers. Little did I think that a year later I would have this lovely baby.*

*Once again my sincere thanks for all your help, and encouragement. My husband can't express how grateful he is to you for all your kindness.*

One of the things I have noticed is that the letters hold up to the mirror to society. Sadly, in recent years, many of my letters reflect the mental health crisis in Ireland. The following gives just one example of it.

*Dear Marion,*

*My late husband always strove for perfection and became frustrated, angry, impatient and intolerant when any signs of imperfection were detectable in anything or in anyone, especially in himself.*

*I loved him to bits but I have to say he had a controlling, aggressive side, which chilled me to the bone, He didn't want me to go out without him and he didn't want my friends in the house. Nothing I did was right and every day it seemed as if I walked on eggshells in case I'd upset him.*

*Things deteriorated alarmingly when my husband started drinking very heavily.*

*There were ever more days when he would pass out and not remember where he had been or where he was. He was arrested for drunk driving and his outbursts frightened the children. He began to threaten death by suicide as, according to him, 'Life was just far too hard.'*

*I overcame my reservation about not speaking openly about my husband and made an appointment to talk with my friend Father Ted – no not the one from the television! He gave me the time and space that enabled me to stand back from the situation and gain a wider perspective on everything. Through my many meetings with him I became strong again and more focused.*

*Five years on myself and my children have made a good recovery in the circumstances but the memory of the fateful day will never leave me.*

*When my husband died he was only forty-three and the children's ages ranged from fourteen to five years. To the outside world it seemed as if he had everything to live for. He had his physical health, he had a wife and six beautiful children, four boys and two girls. He was at the top of his profession and had a big salary.*

*It was a shattering experience. It was news that I had been both dreading and preparing myself to receive for some time. It turned our lives upside down and changed it forever.*

*There seems to be a natural reaction from well-intentioned people who wish to comfort the bereaved, to assume a teacher-student role and to give advice. Such advice can often seem unhelpful to a grieving person. In the shock of loss, those bereaved develop finely tuned antenna for picking up platitudes, which are meant as condolences, but are often perceived as being insults or even self-serving condescendence. I have heard it said that mourning can be a time when the cruellest things are said.*

*I have plenty of advice for those who would like to help a friend who has experienced a bereavement through suicide.*

*I have not passed judgement on my husband, but have commended him in his life and death, to the mercy of God. My faith was a support to me in the dark days but it has been enriched by adversity.*

*Please pray for me and my six children.*

*P.*

These letters also confirm my belief that if you look after people they will look after you. Little things mean a lot and those letters meant something to me. A flower that blooms through adversity is the most rare and beautiful of all.

My heart breaks when I read letters like those. So many young men in particular, who appeared to have so much to live for, but in their last few days they obviously felt they had not enough. How can one make sense of that which defies all sense? All I can do is pay heed to St Paul's advice to the Corinthians, in which he said:

'There must be no passing of premature judgement. Leave that until the Lord comes. He will light up all that is hidden in the dark and reveal the secret intentions of people's hearts.'

I draw strength from my God, who is compassionate, supportive, understanding. He is hard to shock. I guess He's heard it all before. Above all, He is loving. And all He asks is that I love my fellow human beings. I try.

I feel it is a privilege to use my very limited talents to draw attention to the suffering of this world and to strive to bring about change for those who are poor and oppressed. I like to think that they would do the same for me.

Allowing people, especially the suffering, to tell their story at their own pace and without interruption is the best therapy. It is healing and it is on such a basis that real friendship and trust is built.

I have always believed that the capacity to sit back and listen to someone is a huge act of generosity to someone, particularly in times of darkness and distress. I genuinely think that the greatest gift you can give someone is your time.

If you are unlucky enough and if circumstances in life put you down on the gutter, you will never get out of the gutter unless you meet a helping hand; unless you meet somebody who will stick their hand down to you and pull you out of it. That is why the Easter story is so important.

## A Story for All Seasons

The God of the Easter story is an impatient figure, hungry to transform us into worthy bearers of the name 'Christian'. It is through love alone that we please God and our main challenge is to acquire it. Jesus came on earth to love and be loved. The Christian life is an exchange of love – the love we receive and the love we give for Christ. To walk the way of unconditional love is to accept an arduous task.

Jesus did not come to condemn or to pontificate, but to show what it means to be truly human. He came with a promise, 'I come that you may have life and have it to the full.'

Christians best respond to the invitation of Jesus to love not by building memorials to the dead, but by giving food to the living. The secret of life is that only in love for the living is the Spirit praised for ever. Our challenge on Holy Saturday is to allow this love to be a lamp for our steps and a light for our eyes. This is a lull before the Easter storm when we remember our call to bear witness to a Christianity which has a vital, personal quality rather than being something worn ostentatiously like a religious emblem; and a spirituality that is deep, mysterious and beautiful, a religion that gives sympathy to our hearts and understanding to our minds.

Holy Saturday is a day when, more than any other, we are aware of the life that makes us live, the expectation of a new beginning, new birth and hope and the inexhaustible, now accessible divine potential that is all around us. It is a welcome opportunity to savour the energy, joy, and trust of the unique Easter laughter. It is a day when we are particularly conscious of the wisdom of Brendan Kennelly's incisive words, 'Self knows that self is not enough.'

On Holy Saturday we look back at the tyranny of the past, which reached its awful and bloody climax on Good Friday, but we also get a chance to draw breath and reflect on the way Jesus Christ has put our dark past into the perspective of a wondrous future. We prepare ourselves to greet the risen Christ who experienced the fullest joy so that we too could share that glory. Then on Easter Saturday we see Paradise Lost become Paradise Regained.

## A Special Memory

I am not one for making great plans for the future. I am happy to let God surprise me.

In Easter 1993 I was given a gift of a ticket to Rome for the Beatification of the Polish Sister Faustina, after which our pilgrimage would leave immediately for San Giovanni. Because I had said, 'Going to Rome without meeting the Pope would be like going to Mass without receiving Holy Communion,' the former Bishop of Elphin, Dominic Conway, had applied for a privileged place for me at the ceremony, explaining that the nature of my ticket gave me only one day in Rome and stating that I had been cured miraculously at Knock. But he had warned me against any false expectation of meeting the Pope within such a short stay in Rome. The ticket that awaited me from the Vatican on my arrival at our hotel was a ticket to admit me to receive Holy Communion from the Pope. I hadn't asked Bishop Dominic for this. He didn't ask for it. It was only afterwards that he found out that I had asked as a sign from the Lord, as an indication of His approval of my healing ministry, that I should receive Holy Communion from the Pope!

The next chapters of our life I have left in the hands of the Lord. The Lord opened the door, I stepped through the door and kept going. No matter what happens I just take one day at a time. Whatever it brings.

## The God of Small Things

Once there was a great king who was preparing to go to war and he sent his servant to the blacksmith to be certain his horse was ready. The blacksmith told the groom he had no iron to shoe the horse. The king would have to wait. The groom said this was not on and he would make do with what he had. The blacksmith tried his best, but he had not enough iron to correctly fasten the fourth shoe.

The battle began in earnest. The king was leading his troops from the front when his horse's shoe fell off. The horse stumbled and rolled over. The king was thrown to the ground. His men deserted him when they saw his plight. The king was captured and the battle was lost. And all because of a missing nail!

There is a story, too, of the great Irish poet W.B. Yeats, who was going home from work one cold winter's evening. Having failed to find a coat hanger that morning, he had casually thrown his overcoat at the foot of the Abbey Stage. However, when he went back for it that evening, a little kitten had snuggled up inside the coat and was now fast asleep. Rather than disturb the kitten it is said that Yeats went backstage and got a scissors and cut the section of his coat that was sheltering the kitten and headed out in the cold night air with a big hole in his coat!

Little things do mean a lot. We remember that God has showered us with gifts – none more so than when he sent his only Son. Those gifts come with a challenge. Christianity is not about occasional gestures of charity, but about going the second mile, about making choices which involve inconvenience, discomfort and pain.

Few of us have the power to change the world, but we can all do something, albeit something small, to improve life for our neighbour. Today the depth of our commitment to Christ is gauged by the extent to which we love our neighbour – after all, if all we think about is number one, we are not going to add up to very much.

## *Reach Out*

I love Christmas, but it is a time of terrible financial pressure on families, particularly poorer families, some of whom may not yet have paid off the loans they had borrowed the previous Christmas. Advertisements for Christmas gifts, trying to get people to spend money they often don't have, seem to begin earlier and earlier each year. Christmas is the busiest time of the year for retailers, the more we spend the happier the Minister for Finance will be, and Christmas day is not even over when the advertisements for the January sales are beamed into every home.

The true meaning of Christmas is the celebration of the birth, in a field, of the son of a poor carpenter who came to reveal to us the true meaning of life; an all-powerful, all-loving God who came among us, not as a mighty king, with power and wealth, expecting to be served, not as a famous religious guru with a mass following, but as an unknown, powerless infant, totally dependent on the love and care of those around him, whose life and death has revealed to us the true meaning of our own life and death.

One thing I am certain about is that all this pain and suffering and poverty I see so often in my ministry are not caused by God but by us; we are responsible for all this. Believing in a God, for me, it is not just enough to say I believe, but to believe in God means to believe in the dignity of the human person, to look them in the eye, acknowledge them. It is the rejection and self-worth that makes people feel vulnerable, so look that homeless person on the street in the eye and say hello; it could be the one act that makes the difference for them.

## I Have a Dream

I often find myself sad today, listening to the news. In recent years, the issue of housing and homelessness in Ireland has not only reached crisis point but has now been referred as a crisis for so long that our consciences have been anesthetised to its shocking reality. What makes the issue all the more alarming is that the problem seems to be getting worse rather than better.

From the outset, Jesus publicly aligned himself with the poor and the outcasts. Jesus formulated an alternative model of society. Our search for the true face of Christ cannot be authentic until we honestly confront the social structures that cause parents to feel that there is no option for them but to reluctantly send their children into hostel accommodation. It is surely a damning indictment that in the third millennium over three thousand Irish children daily are caught up in the ghastly nightmare of homelessness.

Too often, our Christian traditions have failed in this respect because we have not been part of the solution but through our inaction, or in more traditional terminology 'sins of omission', resolutely remained part of the problem.

The Gospel tells us the story of the rich young man, a good young man, a young man who had kept all the commandments from his youth, whom, nevertheless, could not become a follower of Jesus, could not be admitted to the early Christian community, because his unwillingness to share what he had for the sake of those in need was a contradiction to everything that Jesus lived and preached, an obstacle to revealing a God of compassion by being the compassion of God. In my small way, I want to bring the compassion of God to others.

## Bringing Comfort

Only those who believe in the invisible can do the impossible. By the standards of the world, Jesus was at his most useless on the cross, but it was there that He achieved his greatest glory. The Christian experience is shaped by a particular death, the death of Jesus; His living and dying and rising are the energies that shape our identity. In our suffering we will discover that darkness is the shadow of God's outstretched hand and that a loving God has lowered an arm for us to rest on. That is the God I have experienced and I would like to share this understanding and, in doing so, hopefully comfort those who are suffering.

The Spirit of the Lord is the spirit of truth. A recurring feature of the Christian tradition has been the emergence of prophetic figures who have questioned the ethos and practices of the society.

Religion was a powerful influence for good and for bad in my early life. I often think of those words attributed to Gandhi when he said: 'I like your Christ. I do not like your Christians. Your Christians are not like your Christ.' I suppose for me, listening and observing people, it seems we are great at talking it but not great at living it. I remain a great believer in the philosophy of Christianity.

Like Martin Luther King I have a dream for a just society – one which respects and nurtures all its children equally; insists that people and their human needs are sacrosanct; ensures that its wealth and resources are distributed fairly and equally and guarantees basic human rights for all its people. Perhaps a dream, but, as Abraham Lincoln said, 'The probability that we may fail in the struggle ought not to deter us from the support of a cause we believe to be just.'

Jesus had a dream. His dream was God's dream. He dreamed that all people would live together as one family, God's family. Jesus dreamed of a world where no one would be hungry and have nothing to eat, where no one would be thirsty and have nothing to drink, where no one would be naked and have nothing to wear, where no one would be sick and have no one to visit them, where no one would be in prison and rejected by their community. Jesus was put to death by the religious and political leaders who did not want to see his dream become reality. He was put to death by those who did not want to share their wealth with the poor, by those who wanted to hold on to power for their own self-interests, by those who objected to the tax collectors, the prostitutes and the sinners, refused to associate with them and pushed them to the margins of society. Jesus dreamed that all people would love each other, care for each other, share with each other, respect each other.

We are called to live in dream land, to live in God's dream. A small child, Jesus of Nazareth, born more than two thousand years ago, was then, and is now, the revelation of God's hope for our world. In this child, the human and the divine have become one, for ever inseparable. Other religions might tell us that we encounter God in sacred places, in temples, in places of worship, but we believe that, because of this child Jesus, we encounter God in other human beings. While others might tell us to worship God with sacred actions, with sacrifices, with prayers, Christians, because of this child Jesus, worship by loving God in one another, by caring for, by reaching out to their fellow human beings.

For us to declare ourselves as followers of Jesus is to announce to the world that we have committed our lives to building this dream that Jesus passed on to us. This passion for building a world of justice and peace, in which all people live together as God's people, is the distinguishing characteristic by which Jesus wanted his followers to be identified.

We are called to listen long and hard to the Gospel, to the call of the King who invites us to transform this world through a radical solidarity with all others, to follow Him who gave His life for us by giving our own lives, and everything we have and are, for our brothers and sisters in the court of human suffering.

A community where everyone's needs are met through the caring and sharing of each one in the community, where everyone feels loved, valued and respected, would surely be the Kingdom of God on earth. If Jesus Christ today is to offer hope to those who are struggling, who live on the edge, who feel unwanted, that hope is in people like us.

# 12

# O Happy Day

Perhaps the most exciting event in my 'public life' in recent years was that Knock began the formal process of investigating whether my experience in 1989 constituted an official 'miracle cure'. Under new procedures the case was to be decided in Rome. This development in my story was only possible because, after an arduous struggle, I was finally given access to my medical records through the provisions of the Freedom of Information Act.

Pope John Paul II visited Knock on its centenary in 1979, giving the pilgrim town the ultimate seal of approval from the Church. He famously said:

*'Sé do bheatha, a Mhuire, atá lán de ghrásta . . .*

*'Dear brothers and sisters in Christ, faithful sons and daughters of Mary,*

'Here I am at the goal of my journey to Ireland: the Shrine of Our Lady at Knock. Since I first learned of the centenary of this Shrine, which is being celebrated this year, I have felt a strong desire to come here, the desire to make yet another pilgrimage to the Shrine of the Mother of Christ, the Mother of the Church, the Queen of Peace. Do not be surprised at this desire of mine. It has been my custom to make pilgrimages to the shrines of Our Lady, starting with my earliest youth and in my own country. I made such pilgrimages also as a bishop and as a cardinal. I know very well that every people, every country, indeed every diocese, has its holy places in which the heart of the whole people of God beats, one could say, in more lively fashion: places of special encounter between God and human beings; places in which Christ dwells in a special way in our midst. If these places are so often dedicated to his Mother, it reveals all the more fully to us the nature of his Church. Since the Second Vatican Council, which concluded its Constitution on the Church with the chapter on "The Blessed Virgin Mary, Mother of God, in the Mystery of Christ and of the Church", this fact is more evident for us today than ever—yes, for all of us, for all Christians. Do we not confess with all our brethren, even with those with whom we are not linked in full unity, that we are a pilgrim people? As once this people travelled on its pilgrimage under the guidance of Moses, so we, the People of God of the New Covenant, are travelling on our pilgrim way under the guidance of Christ.

'I am here then as a pilgrim, a sign of the pilgrim Church throughout the world participating, through my presence as Peter's Successor, in a very special way in the centenary celebration of this Irish Shrine at Knock.

'"Blessed are you among women, and blessed is the fruit of your womb!" This is also my greeting to *Muire Máthair Dé*, Mary the Mother of God, Queen of Ireland, at this Shrine of Knock. With these words, I want to express the immense joy and gratitude that fills my heart today in this place. I could not have wanted it any differently.

Highlights of my recent pastoral journeys have been the visits to the Shrines of Mary: to Our Lady of Guadalupe in Mexico, to the Black Madonna of Jasna Góra in my homeland, and three weeks ago to Our Lady of Loreto in Italy. Today I come here because I want all of you to know that my devotion to Mary unites me, in a very special way, with the people of Ireland.'

Although many cures have been associated with the shrine at Knock over the years, it never had a proclaimed miracle. In 1984 a new Knock Shrine Medical Bureau was set up to establish if cures claimed in Knock, Co. Mayo, are medical or miracle. It was immediately described as a 'miracle bureau', one whose objective was to rigorously examine claims of cures. The bureau consisted of a team of doctors headed by Fr Michael Casey, a retired professor of chemistry at Maynooth University, and a Dominican priest.

In the Knock Shrine on the first of September 2019 a bishop has said I was 'healed' during a pilgrimage to Knock thirty years ago. It is the first time the Catholic Church has said a pilgrim was cured at Ireland's National Marian Shrine at Knock. Francis Duffy, the Bishop of Ardagh and Clonmacnois, described my healing as something which 'defies medical explanation'.

Speaking in Knock, Bishop Duffy said:

> 'I recognise that Marion was healed from her long-standing illness while on pilgrimage in this sacred place. Marion's healing is life-changing. Many have attested to the dramatic change that came about in Marion here and on her return to Athlone in 1989. It is also a healing for which there is no medical explanation at present, it is definite and yet defies medical explanation.'

Also speaking in Knock that day, the Archbishop of Tuam Dr Michael Neary said:

> 'Today the Church formally acknowledges that this healing does not admit of any medical explanation and joins in prayer, praise and thanksgiving to God. In these situations the Church must always be very cautious. This is illustrated by the fact that thirty years have elapsed since this took place, during which time the examination by the Medical Bureau [at the Knock shrine] testifies that there is no medical explanation for this healing.'

Why did it take thirty years for them to formally recognise my cure? For many years, the medical view stated that no definite diagnosis of my condition was available, leading the Church authorities to adopt a wait-and-see attitude to my claim. The file on my case was reviewed in my presence in January 2019 by, among others, my local bishop Francis Duffy of Ardagh and Clonmacnois, Archbishop Dr Michael Neary of Tuam, in whose diocese Knock is located, two priests and my husband Jimmy. A letter from a consultant gastroenterologist stating that, having reviewed my medical file, 'regardless of whether her condition is organic or psychological, the dramatic improvement from the time of her visit to Knock is unexplained'.

The consultant added, 'My feeling is that her improvement is very unlikely to be explained by conventional medical wisdom.' A consultant neurologist who reviewed my file stated that 'it would be fair to say she has been cured of neurological symptoms but not of MS. It seems to me that Mrs Carroll had medically unexplained symptoms which have now (thankfully) resolved.'

So how did it all come to this?

## Knock

Knock's setting, itself a love letter from God, opens pilgrims' eyes to the natural beauty and splendour of the world that surrounds them, inspiring them with a new confidence and passion for life, and helping them to confront key thresholds of human experience. Those who come to visit quietly marvel at the never-ending wonder of a God who created such diversity in life and this in turn has enabled them to observe the miracle that insight and awareness could create within them. It helps people to appreciate the words of the German mystic Meister Eckhart: 'One must not always think so much about what one should do, but rather what one should be. Our works do not ennoble us; but we must ennoble our works.'

For some who find the Church irrelevant to their hopes, fears, creative longings, and often desperate struggles or those who experience disillusionment, confusion and anger in the face of what they perceive as closed, dry and dogmatic ecclesiastical attitudes, Knock has been an oasis and opened up the vista to a world 'charged with the grandeur of God'. It has been a magnet for those who sense the stirrings of a new beginning within them and their communities. They have been drawn to it by the possibilities it offers for spiritual growing, for fresh visions and for imaginative networking. It has brought hope and joy to many bewildered and despondent souls and allowed them to be caught up in the wonder of the divine and held in God's limitless embrace, as looking for and longing for God regularly is what our hearts most desire.

Knock has been a sanctuary that illuminates visitors' minds to see beauty, their desires to seek possibility and their hearts to love life. It enables them to experience a true sense of belonging in this often-troubled world and a gentle gift of light in their paths through this earthly existence. Knock has helped many to find harmony between their faith and their lives and involvement in the world and to spend time developing a personal and progressively deeper relationship with God in Jesus Christ.

*Welcome*

In 2018 there was a real buzz in Knock when it emerged that Pope Francis was coming to the shrine. There were great preparations beforehand steered by Fr Richard Gibbons, the parish priest of Knock. I had a tiny part to play in my role as a *Cairde Mhuire*, previously known as handmaids.

On the journey, in thinking about what he wanted to say to the Irish people, the Pope found himself thinking about the Church of San Damiano. Towards the end of 1205, Francis of Assisi had an encounter there which had a profound impact on him. The church was officiated by a poor priest who could not even afford to buy oil to light the lamp in front of a Byzantine image of the crucified Christ. Francis was captivated by this crucifix. It spoke to him: 'Go Francis and repair my house which, as you see, is falling into ruin.'

St Francis forcefully reminds us that all of God's people are called to repair God's house, as it falls into disrepair. One of his key messages for all of us today is that we must play our part in healing the wounds of the past.

Pope Francis thought that he should tell the Church in Ireland that it must reach out, as both Jesus and St Francis did, to those in agony with empathy so that we can give adequate witness to the suffering Christ who never failed to show extraordinary tenderness to the damaged, the despairing and the distressed.

St Francis does offer a blueprint for the future of the Church. His Church will not be built on great cathedrals because that is not where its founder would have gone. On a holy night Jesus was born almost unnoticed in a sleepy stable in Bethlehem. On Easter Sunday morning he returned once again into our world like a thief in the night, noticed only by a woman who was scorned and ridiculed by a judgemental society. This new Church will be based on such humility. It will call for new attitudes, new structures and new heroes.

Such a journey will require courage, but this is a time for bravery. St Francis knew what it was like to go outside his comfort zone. Often he would ride his horse in the plain below Assisi, where there was a leper colony. It was on one of these occasions that he met a leper face to face. Although being terrified of the poor man, Francis dismounted from his horse and ran towards him, offering him money, and the kiss of peace. He would cherish this encounter all his life and brought it to his memory before his death. St Francis is a prophetic presence who challenges us to change our world today and for each of us to be 'the herald of the great king'.

St Francis famously said that it is in giving that we receive. He did more than alert and alarm anyone willing to listen. He embodied what is best in us all because he lived by the motto that giving in its purest form expects nothing in return.

Pope Francis came with that powerful message. However, when he blessed the Mayo jersey all the Mayo fans hoped he would bring a miracle of his own and that Mayo would finally win the All-Ireland!

## Speedy

The story was that Pope Francis was so excited about his visit to Ireland for the World Meeting of Families that he decided to visit the Irish College in Rome to learn a few words in Irish. Not a man to bother with formalities, Pope Francis told his driver that he would drive himself and he instructed his driver to take his place in the back seat.

Pope Francis was getting so absorbed by thinking about his speech that he completely forgot about the speed limit. That all changed when an angry-looking policeman pulled up beside him on his motorcycle and waved him down. Pope Francis was a little surprised that instead of approaching his car the policeman spoke into his phone. The cop explained to his boss that he had pulled over a dignitary for speeding but he did not think it would be wise to charge him.

The chief of police asked. 'Who have you got there, a Member of Parliament?'

The traffic cop replied, 'Bigger.'

Chief: 'Not the President?'

The traffic cop replied, 'Bigger.'

'Well,' said the chief, 'Tell me who is it then, for God's sake?'

Traffic cop: 'Well that's just it. I think it is God.'

Chief: 'Why do you say that?'

Traffic cop: 'Well, he's got Pope Francis as his chauffeur!'

More seriously though, Pope Francis came to Ireland with a rich vision. In 2014–2015, the year of Consecrated Life, Pope Francis issued his memorable exhortation to the religious that speaks equally to lay people: 'The Church must be attractive. Wake up the world. Be witnesses of a different way of acting, of living. It is possible to live differently in this world. It is this witness I expect from you.'

### A New Community

The human person is a unity rather than a duality of spirit and body. The process of humanisation is an integral part of spiritual development. A communal model images our relationship with God in the context of a community of faith. The Spirit speaks through all, and we grow in our faith life with, in, and through others. We are one body.

The Bible tells us that there are a variety of gifts, but the same spirit and there are varieties of service, but the same Lord; and there are varieties of working but it is the same God who inspires them in everyone. This recognition led to a revolution in the understanding of spirituality – from 'other-worldly' to 'this-worldly', a genuine apostolic spirituality which recognises that Christians work out their salvation by involvement in the human struggle for justice and peace. Spirituality is understood as the experience of consciously striving to integrate one's life in terms not of isolation and self-absorption but of self-transcendence toward the ultimate value one perceives.

The Second Vatican Council put a lot of emphasis on freedom and personal autonomy but some Catholics experienced this as a mixed blessing. The idea of having to decide for oneself, as Dostoevsky's poem within *The Brothers Karamazov* 'The Grand Inquisitor' suggests, can be too great a burden for many people. If you have doubts all, you need do is to refer to the relevant authority. The Council put a very big emphasis on personal development and a leadership policy. Practical changes were introduced to give outward expression to this new understanding; for example, Church appointments were no longer made by letter but after consultation. There was a determined effort not to repeat the sins of the past and put square pegs in round holes, and a greater attention was paid to the affective. The clergy and members of religious congregations went on a range of courses. Prayer life changed. A lot of litanies were dropped and individuals took more responsibility for their own spiritual sustenance.

Outside influences, such as the charismatic renewal movement, began to seep through. Outsiders were engaged by the religious to bring new insights to scripture and this opened up a new world of personal development. A unity of believers that had been achieved in an external sense was replaced by a unity of conviction based on consensus and expressed through free and personal faith.

There was also a much more dynamic understanding of morality: a move away from an excessive emphasis on sin and rules, and a new focus on a passionate love of God. Thus, the new pilgrim community will develop the full range of our capacities for loving to empower us to become transparent, more vividly sacramental of God's love. St Augustine recognised this in his famous dictum: 'Thou hast made us for thyself O God, and our hearts cannot rest until they rest in thee.'

This new community will commit to St Augustine's idea of 'mingling mercy with misery'. It will not simply preach compassion, but live it. It will make personal, intimate contact with the rejected ones: the homeless, the imprisoned, the sick, the dying, the old and the lonely. The world desperately needs to be taught that compassion is needed everywhere, in our own society, in our own communities. We all have marginalised and rejected people.

Love is at the very heart of the Christian life. After all, as we find in the first letter of St John, love is even God's definition. Christians are not simply God's possessions, but in a sense God's partners in loving. The pilgrim Church that Pope Francis wants us to become will care for the most damaged and show us what the kingdom is. God has showered us with gifts – none more so than when he sent his only Son. Those gifts come with a challenge. This can be seen at the beginning of C.S. Lewis's Narnia books, where the Beaver makes the point repeatedly that Aslan is not a tame lion. The lion has a challenging, even dark, side as well as a comforting one.

But this Christian love is a lamp for our steps and a light for our eyes. To see ourselves as being separate from God and from each other is an illusion. We are all connected to one another and if someone performs an unkind act then it, too, has an effect on us all. At the end of our lives we want to be able to say that somehow we brought the compassion of God to people. The Church of the future will be an oasis of love to a troubled world.

There is a sense from Pope Francis of being challenged to live a much deeper Christian life with God at the centre and a recognition that to be a Christian today is to answer the call to be our best selves, to be fully human. Out of that, the Church will empower lay people to enable the kingdom to come and to journey with people through their lives. It will instil a very strong communal desire to be prophets, a sense of being called to reveal God in some way and a belief that if we fail to do that then we fail the world. In that way it will unequivocally take the side of the downtrodden, the oppressed and the marginalised.

Can the same be said of us now? Whose side are we on? What price are we willing to pay for championing unpopular causes or standing up for what we know to be right?

The pilgrim Church will challenge us to rediscover our prophetic role as Christians, a quality of life which attempts to give renewed heart to the Christian life by a radical commitment to simplicity, sharing and intimacy. It will agree instinctively with the call of Jesus to his followers to walk the way of humility and not to be seduced by the false gods of power and arrogance.

Often we live with the tension of Mary and Martha in the Gospel, between the active and the contemplative. However, it is not a case of 'either/or' but 'both/and'. We need to complement our prayer with practical action because as St Francis of Assisi forcefully rings the bell to us: 'The cloister is the world.'

In 1993 Pope John Paul II responded to a question posed at the Second Parliament of Religions in Chicago about why there were so many different religions:

'You speak of many religions. Instead I will attempt to show the common fundamental element and the common root of these religions. Instead of marvelling at the fact that Providence allows such a great variety of religions, we should be amazed at the number of common elements found within them.'

While Pope John Paul II was, of course, not saying that all religions are the same, he did say that they have a common root. In this respect he was closely following the teaching of the Second Vatican Council, which had a major concern for world peace. The Council was acutely aware that there could be no world peace while there was hostility between the world religions.

The triumvirate of dialogue, reconciliation and conversion of heart will be ongoing processes for the pilgrim Church. Results will not be instantaneous. This journey towards a grand and shared narrative will inevitably face many setbacks. In the words of St Catherine of Siena:

> 'To the servant of God, every place is the right place,
> And every time is the right time.
> We are of such value to God
> That He came to love among us.'

If we are really interested in the salvation of our troubled world we must persist on this difficult journey. Given what Pope John Paul II called 'our culture of death' and the prevalence of violence, poverty, injustice, racism, prejudice and intolerance anything that brings us even a small step closer to peace must be vigorously pursued. Pope Francis's Church of the future will not simply talk about peace and justice. It will actively lead the charge. Please God I can play my own small part in helping the dream of Pope Francis to come true.

Thankfully – given the recognition of my 'miracle cure' – I can now do so with the knowledge that I have the public support of the Church behind me.


*Return Trip*

In September 2019, almost thirty years to the day when my cure happened, I went back to Knock. This time I was in a very different place physically and emotionally. It was a very different feeling because they were going to be making a bit of a fuss over me.

Leading his diocese's annual pilgrimage to Knock Basilica, Bishop Duffy announced to the congregation, which included myself, Jimmy, our children and other relatives, that he did not doubt that 'there was a healing, a cure of the illness that beset Marion for several years'.

One thing that had worked in my favour in terms of my cure being officially recognised by the Catholic Church was that, in 2009 the then manager of Knock Shrine, Pat Lavelle, and the then chief steward, Tom Neary, compiled a series of eyewitness statements to the events of the day of my cure to help advance my case. They took formal statements from a number of people who were involved on the day. I am very grateful to both Pat and Tom for their help in this way and for their consistent support down the years. I am also grateful to those who gave their testimonies, which helped clarify the extent of the dramatic change that came over me that day. The following three statements give a flavour of these testimonies.

*Eyewitness Statement – Sadie Feeley*
My name is Sadie Feeley and I live in Barrybeg, Athlone, and I'm relating what happened on the day Marion Carroll was cured in September 1989. I'm a handmaid at Knock, so on the first Sunday of every month it would be my job to get to Knock by nine a.m. and on that Sunday morning I did as I do every first Sunday I went to Knock...

I was there making up the beds when this invalid was wheeled into me [on the stretcher trolley] and there was just the two of us there, she was the first invalid in. I went over and I greeted her, asked her who she was and where she came from. I was surprised that she was from Athlone because I am from Athlone and we hadn't met before, so we exchanged chat about where she lived and where I lived and what was wrong with her and a few other particularities about her sickness and what would happen during the day, although mind you now she knew a little about Knock because she had been there several times.

So we proceeded then to prepare for the day. We didn't go out in the morning. We stayed on in the First Aid. I had nursing duties to perform with Marion, which I found very difficult because her speech was very impaired. She didn't have anything to eat, but then her swallow was affected so that probably was why. At about two o'clock we went to the basilica for the Anointing of the Sick and the Mass. Now at this stage I don't remember anything spectacular about the Anointing of the Sick...

The sick would be brought from all the hospitals in the diocese, which resulted in some of them being in wheelchairs. As a matter of fact, I don't remember any stretcher only Marion's, and that was especially awkward and especially adapted to suit her sickness. I remember it still it had a huge head frame which kept her head stable. I remember that very well, I remember being told to make sure that the head cage was always there.

I don't remember very much about the Anointing and then Mass started at three o'clock. Now I wasn't standing beside Marion all the time because there would be other invalids fairly near you and if they wanted any assistance you'd be ready to go to them because Marion was strapped to her stretcher. She'd be fairly safe, but the others were able to move around so you always had to keep a watchful eye over what was going on around.

I remember Mass, I remember Mass fairly well even to this day. I remember still where Marion was during Mass. I just don't remember anything really about the Mass until it came to Communion and I remember I was very near Marion at that time and she received Holy Communion and she said to me I remember this very distinctly, she said to me, 'I swallowed Communion and I haven't swallowed for a long time, I haven't taken Communion.'

I don't know what way it was put to me, but I knew it was something different and she said on top of that she said, 'I swallowed Communion but I got a pain in my heel' and she said, 'It's a long time since I felt pain but I very definitely got a pain in my heel when I received Communion today.'

I remember that very well. I think I might remember it all my life about how definite she was about this pain in her heel, that had no feeling in her heel for I don't know how many years. Now I don't know and remember much more . . . until back in the care centre and we were having tea and now these are my memories and mine only.

Mrs Coyne (the chief handmaid) came along visiting all the invalids and I was standing near Marion. Now I was keeping a watchful eye on others as well and Mrs Coyne gave Marion *The Knock Annual*. It opened on a page when she left it down on her chest or her body and the page said the Family Rosary. Mrs Coyne said to her, 'Do you say the Rosary, Marion?' and she said 'I have never missed a Rosary, myself and Jimmy since the day we were married,' and she said, 'When Jimmy went to the Lebanon, he said the Rosary every day in the Lebanon and I in Athlone at four p.m.' Now I recall that very distinctly and Mrs Coyne said to her, 'You must have a very good husband,' and she said, 'Jimmy is wonderful.'

I know Marion said to me, 'I think I could stand if somebody would let me off this trolley.' Well, I said to myself, 'Sadie, this is where you move back now because if you let Marion off that trolley and she falls off you'll be blamed,' so I got out of the way. I stepped back. Now we would always be trained like that as nurses: that if there was anything you knew that was unusual, to step out of the limelight, let in the doctors or someone else unless you were bold enough to take responsibility. I remember distinctly stepping back and I think it was Mrs O'Meara that came forward and she opened the straps [of the stretcher] and Marion got out on the floor and all I can remember is her standing and I remember her standing back into the trolley and someone said to her, 'Are you not staying up?' and she said, 'I don't want to stay up. I know now that I can stand and that's all I want, the rest will come.'

Now I know there was a lot of commotion then after that. People were all coming in on top of her. Word spread around that someone had got out of their trolley and stood up to walk and had walked. Then I said, 'I have to go because I'll be locked in St John's for the night if I don't get out of here.' Marion, you see, was going home in the ambulance. I wasn't going home in the ambulance, so I remember saying to her, 'I'll go to the house when I get to Athlone,' and she said, 'Do.' Now, her speech had improved and everything at this stage.

So I went to the house when I got to Athlone, it could be seven o'clock then maybe, maybe after it. When I went to the house, Marion was in bed which I must say disappointed me, so I waited on then and I said, 'Marion, why are you in bed?' and she said to me, 'For the simple reason that I'm tired,' which was a very appropriate answer after the day she'd had.


*Eyewitness Statement – Nuala O'Meara*

I went to Knock with my husband and he was medical officer of the pilgrimage. We were seated in the four seats behind the altar and I noticed a patient coming in on a stretcher and I remarked to my husband that it was Marion. I knew who she was and it wasn't until after Mass when the patients were brought down to St John's, where they usually have a cup of tea and that, that I went to speak to Marion.

I asked her how she was, she acknowledged me and knew me and she did say to me would I open her straps, so I said to Marion, 'I'm not a nurse,' and I said, 'We better ask a nurse.' I asked Nurse Maureen Rafferty and I think Sr Antonio was there.

Maureen opened the straps and Marion walked. She got up and stood up and she wanted to move. We were inclined to help her and support her but she said, 'No.' She wanted to move herself and somebody produced a chair and I suppose from here to the wall or that, I'm not sure how many feet, but she did, she managed to get over the chair.

She had a cup of tea given to her. I'm not quite sure who gave it to her, after I wasn't near enough to her. I think a few people came around and were surprised to see what had happened.

## *Eyewitness Statement — Joseph Quinn*

Other people to give their statements included Monsignor Joseph Quinn, the then Parish Priest of Knock, the Rector of Knock Shrine and the Episcopal Vicar for Knock Shrine and Parish. He stated:

> 'She is in my opinion, a most genuine, sincere and authentic woman. Her recovery on that day of grace in 1989 has been persistent and she enjoys good health to this day. She is a great Ambassador for Knock, all over Ireland and abroad and I believe that she is a chosen instrument of God and Our Lady to communicate the message of Knock's apparition to others, at home and abroad.'

## *Big News*

I knew that the decision was made to make my cure official back in January 2019. They decided to hold over the announcement until the thirtieth anniversary in September. That was the hardest part because I could not tell my family in case the word leaked out. All my friends who came thought they were coming to celebrate the thirtieth anniversary of my cure. They all got a huge shock when the announcement was made.

It was so lovely to have all my family involved in the ceremony. Jimmy was involved in his role as a *Cairde Mhuire*. For years, his particular role as a steward has been to carry the canopy for the

Blessed Sacrament in the procession. My children, Cora and Anthony, and grandchildren Chantel, Faith, Bethany, James and Ben were involved in bringing up the gifts. Some of my dear friends did the readings. The choir of St Mel's cathedral did truly beautiful singing. Anne Marie Duggan-Hayes did the responsorial psalm. It was great to be able to invite those who have helped me down the years; those like the representatives of the people of Offaly who, when I was very sick, sent me to Lourdes, and those from Cloghan who got me an electric wheelchair when I was at my very lowest. There were people from England and other places, too.

My good friend David Parkes came from Medjugorje to sing '*Ave Maria*'. Like me, David Parkes stared death in the face. The victim of severe Crohn's disease, he had undergone ten major bowel operations and the medical team working on his case had made it clear there was nothing more they could do for him. Weighing 110 pounds, in constant pain and suffering, he prepared to die. An invitation was issued to David and his wife, Anne, to visit Medjugorje where alleged apparitions of the Blessed Virgin were reportedly taking place. Not overly interested in religion, David agreed to go see the country where he had spent his honeymoon, considering it his last vacation. There, David very reluctantly attended a healing Mass being conducted by the renowned healing priest, Fr Peter Rookey. On his return to Ireland, Peter showed no further symptoms of Crohn's disease and years later he continues to be free of this deadly disease.

## A Beautiful Homily

I was asked afterwards how I felt about the occasion. It was kind of like my wedding. It was all about me and yet it was not mine. Bishop Francis said beautiful things in his homily to publicly announce and acknowledge my healing at the national Marian shrine. On what he described as 'a very special day for Knock and for the Church in Ireland and further afield...' he said that, 'A lot of good will come from this. Your story and your healing will bring hope and a strengthening of faith to my people.'

The focal point of the Mass was that wonderful and generous homily from Bishop Francis. He went on to say:

'Good afternoon everyone and welcome to the 2019 Ardagh and Clonmacnois Diocesan Pilgrimage to Our Lady's Shrine. I welcome all who have travelled from the various parishes of the diocese and all those who have come from other places in Ireland, and from abroad, to be with us today... A special welcome to Marion Carroll and her husband Jimmy and their family and friends. Today is a special anniversary for Marion, the thirtieth anniversary of her healing while on this pilgrimage in 1989. We gather as pilgrims in this place that is sacred to so many, we make our journey, maybe we bear the needs of others with us but is our personal journey, and it is very special because of that. Today we hold in our prayers our family members, friends and those who have used for our prayers. We ask the Lord's pardon and his peace...

'Today, this is a very special Diocesan Pilgrimage to Knock. Thirty years ago to the day, on this pilgrimage, on the first Sunday in September 1989, Marion Carroll was healed... I recognise that Marion was healed from her long-standing illness while on pilgrimage in this sacred place. Marion's healing is good news for her, for her husband Jimmy, for her family and friends...

'Today we acknowledge the Lord's work, through the intercession of Mary. Today we give thanks to God for this healing, a healing within the tradition and practice of Jesus when He walked this earth, and healing that has continued since then.

'The apparition at Knock one hundred and forty years ago was a silent one, no words were spoken. Many people like that unique feature of this Marian apparition. St John holding the book of the gospels points to the importance of the Word of God. God speaks to us in Scripture. God uses us, uses you and me to be channels of his Healing to other people.

'God uses our silence. The silence of being there, being with, comfortable and comforting, being a balm for others, reminiscent of the apparition of Knock itself, no words, no sounds, silent and being present, Mary, St Joseph, St John, the Lamb of God, the Angels of the Altar. Sometimes words can get in the way, they may not be needed, just being with someone who is ill, hurting, anxious can be enough to usher in peace and calm, the balm of being with it and accompanying.

'We all like to be recognised, praised and thanked and given a boost by what people say to us. We can use our words to do great things for others. One of the great things we can do is use words that give freedom. Jesus spoke about visiting prisoners – setting prisoners free – those imprisoned by the opinion of others, by inadequacies, imprisoned by petty issues or by great matters. Pope Francis wrote about words that judge others. The Holy Father said, "The Lord asks us above all not to judge and not to condemn. If anyone wishes to avoid God's judgement, he should not make himself the judge of his brother or sister. Human beings, whenever they judge, look no farther than the surface, whereas the Father looks into the very depths of the soul."

'Many feel lonely or troubled and have a great need to talk to someone they can trust and who will listen. The opportunity to do so can often be the difference between despair and hope. Certainly, we can help free people, help them grow and flourish, by the careful and gentle use of words that lift up, that build confidence and that can open up hope. The Lord can work through our words to heal.

'I mention the gentle use of words. Our first reading, from the Book of Ecclesiasticus says, "be gentle in carrying out your business". Gentleness is a wonderful quality to have, it can be a means of touching another, accepting them, making them feel at home and needed and valued. Mentioning "gentle", I mention that gentle man, Jimmy, Marion's husband. Jimmy is referred to as Marion's "beacon". The Lord also works through you, Jimmy, and through many others.

'Today is an occasion to have a great joy and thanksgiving to God for healing Marion. It is also an occasion to be thankful to God for the good that Marion has carried out over many years in His name.

'Amen.'


*Hair-raising*

A priest asked me afterwards if I was worried about it beforehand.

I replied: 'I was only worried about one thing, Father.'

'What's that,' he replied?

'I haven't got a model figure. What was I going to wear?'

You have to have a sense of humour. God has to have a sense of humour the things he makes us go through.

Shortly after my cure I put some colour in my hair and I met a priest I knew well, but he did not recognise me. I said, 'Are you not talking to me, Father?'

He said, 'What did you do to your hair?'

I answered, 'You might be the very man to help me out. Would you know the name of Our Lady's hairdresser? She has a different colour hair in every apparition!'

# 13

# Set Free for Freedom

*'The only real mistake is the one*
*from which we learn nothing.'*

— HENRY FORD

People think that the announcement that my cure was finally recognised officially by the Catholic Church was the biggest event in my life in the last few years. They are wrong. Of course it was lovely, but only people who have been through what I have been through can understand this. The big event for me, in fact, was that after a lengthy battle I was finally given access to my medical records in 2015.

That struggle was very frustrating. There were some tough moments on the way. I watched a television documentary about Knock and my story was a central part. I was in a state of total incredulity when I watched someone talking about my medical records without having asked my permission to do so. The frustration was intensified that this was happening at a time when I did not have access to them myself.

I have no idea who it was that introduced the Freedom of Information Act in Ireland, but I have reason to be very thankful to them. It was through that mechanism that I was finally able to get access to my medical records.

As I have previously alluded to, prior to my diagnosis, I was in a bad way. One of the doctors I had dealt with had implied that I had a mental illness. I grew up in Athlone when there was a huge stigma attached to mental illness. Thankfully that is changing, but we still have a long way to go in that respect.

I was bruised, battered and broken because of my physical state, but that doctor's implication that I was mentally ill was the wound that cut the deepest. I took it to heart and it left a huge physic scar on my consciousness for over thirty years. I know that people will find this hard to believe, but I was always brought up to believe that 'doctor knows best' and I believed deep down that he must be right. So I had a deep-rooted, enduring fear for almost thirty years after my cure that I had some kind of 'problem'. I lived in a constant fear that sometime somebody was going to come along and take me away.

I kept this fear to myself, because my emotional state was so frail at that time when that doctor told me that I was mentally ill that it developed a vice-like grip on me which I was unable to shake off. Finally though, when I did get my medical records, I saw that a psychiatrist had written shortly after that doctor had given his damning verdict that I was 'happily married and well-balanced'.

I could scarcely believe my eyes. Tears toppled in steady streams down my cheeks.

If I had only been told that thirty years earlier, I would have escaped all that torment wondering if I had a serious mental health issue.

I had lived in a prison, without walls, for over thirty years.

And it was all unnecessary.

I can't describe the enormous weight that was lifted off my shoulders when I read those words.

The closest I can come to is:

*Total liberation.*
*At last.*

Finally I can make St Teresa of Avila's prayer my own:

> *'Let nothing disturb you*
> *Let nothing frighten you*
> *All things are passing away*
> *God never changes*
> *Patience obtains all things*
> *She who possesses God lacks nothing*
> *God alone suffices.'*

From a more personal perspective my family life has been even more thrilling.

I have seen my two children give me five wonderful grandchildren. Cora has three fantastic daughters: Chantel, Faith and Bethany. Anthony has two great sons: James and Ben. My grandchildren's ages range from the mid-teens to early twenties. Anthony is living in Galway, which is not that far away. Cora lives like me in Athlone, but she is in Connacht and I am in Leinster! She lives in Saint Anne's, beside where I was born – so it is lovely that the wheel has turned the full circle for the family.

## The Ambassador

Since I got married I have never needed a guardian angel. Jimmy has been mine. Going on forty-eight years now, we are still best friends.

Jimmy has found a new role in recent years. He has become an unofficial ambassador.

To Santa Claus!

From August Jimmy now grows a beard and in the run-up to Christmas he dresses up in the red costume and looks exactly like Santa Claus. He carefully co-ordinates with the parents of a number of children and appears to them on FaceTime.

The children are convinced that he is Santa Claus and think this is the greatest thing ever. The parents are delighted, too, because Jimmy always checks in with them in advance, so when he asks them if they have been good children he always has something specific to say for them like, 'I heard you broke your brother's bicycle.' When he says this their eyes nearly pop out of their heads!

After those conversations the children really embrace the message: 'You better watch out you better not cry!'

So, this makes their parents very happy as well as the children.


*Heartbreak*

Into every life some rain must fall. While I have known the best of times, I have also known the worst of times.

Some years ago, I was in Birmingham for a family wedding. I was worried about my mother because she had asthma and other medical problems and was on an oxygen machine. I rang my father one night to check that she was still okay. The next day I rang Jimmy and he said, 'I'm awful sorry, your father has died.' I instinctively said, 'Jimmy, you mixed them up. It's my mother.' However, my father had in fact died from a heart attack.

Good habits are learned young. I was immersed into a value system from an early age that largely remains with me to the present day. If a child is made to feel loved and wanted they will develop a positive self-image and will in turn be able to form good relationships with others. If, on the other hand, the child is neglected, ignored or abused verbally, physically or emotionally they will develop a low self-image which will have negative and detrimental effects on relationships for the rest of their lives.

My father was a good man. He had a blending of strength and good nature that tends to make respect and affection come in a single flood. He believed that to have respect from those that know you is the greatest honour of all. I think that is a good philosophy to live your life by. He was a man of principle, a believer that some general notion of decency is essential to walk the path of life. The most important people in his life were his wife and his children.

Dad needed to support his instinctive certainty with a deep under-standing of the traditional imperatives of family life. Part of this was that he had a healthy scepticism about his own importance.

He was not a man whose utterances suggested a mere nodding acquaintance with everyday reality or one who had to peer through the cloud of self-absorption to face the world. He was a private man, living a public life by virtue of his job. His rich wellspring of humanity prevented him from raising a moat against the outside world. He had an authority about him. He was not the most tall man, but it was not his physical presence that did it. Nor was it that he spoke voluminously or loudly. What drew people to him was something intangible. By instinct he had an exceptionally firm grasp of human psychology and how to appeal to it. He was a Renaissance-like figure with an engaging sense of humour, a healthy dose of modesty and an enormous appetite for life.

On the day of his funeral I took time to look around at my family. They were suffering so much, too. I knew then that I would have to come to terms with the sadness of his death, if only to help the other family members at least so that they could pick up the pieces of their lives and try to cope as best they could.

I waited until the mourners had departed to be alone with him for a final moment. I prayed to buy him some shares in the hereafter. Now I know why 'goodbye' is the most painful word in the English language. Parting is no sweet sorrow.

Not long after Dad died, I was visiting my mother one night. It was the day before my birthday. She said, 'Do you know that at twelve tomorrow all those years ago I nearly died giving birth to you?' I told her that we would wrap her up and take her out to lunch the next day at twelve noon. What we weren't to know then was that she would die at midday that following day. It was very tough and a really sad time in my life.

However, I believe happiness is linked to simplicity. If we got a bottle of lemonade as children we thought life did not get better than this. The more complicated life gets, the less happy people are because their expectations soar. What is learned in childhood is engraved in stone. I learned the virtues of thrift and stoicism at an early age. Poverty, even relative poverty, makes you clever. Without some ingenuity you do not get to eat all the time, and so you have to be smart. Potatoes are peeled slowly and methodically with a small paring knife, leaving as little potato on the peel as possible. Simple things, but look after the pennies and the shillings and pounds take care of themselves.

My mind is a theatre of happy memories that make up the landscape of my childhood, particularly of my parents, who had a decisive influence on my life, leaving a warm afterglow to light up numerous conversations years later. I am deeply appreciative of the self-sacrificing efforts which my parents made for their children. My mother was one of those women who had a natural refinement and strength of character that no university education could provide. My mother was our home. I could not imagine it without her. She was kind and loving when it was needed; she was supportive when support was required and she could be strict when discipline was called for. Above all, she could be great craic. Like many of her era, she was blessed with a wonderful memory. You could even say she was a bit of a historian. She enriched our lives with all the local history and much folklore and the odd sprinkle of gossip.

She had no idea of the notions of evil or dishonesty. She loved without precondition or qualification and drew love from others like a magnet and radiated love to those she knew like an open fire. She was the heart of her family because she generous to a fault and possessed a great sense of humour, flavoured with a sharp wit. There was never a dull moment when she was centre stage. The memory of her lingers for life in my mind and in the minds of those who grew up with her.

Whenever it was necessary, my mother had no hesitation in bringing me down a peg or two, but criticism was always tactfully offered. In the cossetted comfort of her presence, I learned much about patience, kindness and selflessness. She had a presence you can experience, but not hope to define. Whenever I think of her, childhood memories strike me with the suddenness of an avalanche.

When I remember my parents' influence, a verse I learned as a girl in school comes back to me like an old friend:

'Beautiful faces are they that wear
The light of a pleasant spirit there;
Beautiful hands are they that do
Deeds that are noble, good and true;
Beautiful feet are they that go
Swiftly to lighten another's woe.'

Nothing can ever be the same again, but we are all doing the best we can to live through the family celebrations as they come along – without them. All the Christmases and birthdays too.

My parents are the ghosts I carry around within me. It comforted me to think that the two of the most important people ever in my life lay side-by-side. For a moment I longed to be with both of them – but my time had not yet come.

Now 'coming home' will always be a sad occasion for me. I called in to say goodbye to them in their room. How could someplace so familiar become so alien? Their ghost whispered from every corner. Every piece of furniture has its unique memory of them.

Without my parents the world is a poorer place.

I have also lost most of my aunts and uncles. I am the oldest survivor in my father's family. I have only one surviving uncle on my mother's side, and that is hard.

The other great sadness in my life came when my beautiful daughter Cora was diagnosed with MS in the early 2000s. I knew she had it well before the diagnosis. An outsider would not be aware that she has the condition, but someone who has MS would spot the signs very quickly. The big advance for Cora compared to when I was waiting for a diagnosis has been the advent of MRI scans. She is doing fine, thanks to the drugs regime she is on.

### Goodbye to You, My Trusted Friend

I have also lost a good friend. Another Athlone resident was the great showband icon from the 1960s, Doc Carroll. He ensured his immortality with his classic version of 'Old Man Trouble' that sent many a jiving couple home sweating after a night out.

Doc was a great pal of mine. He had a very strong faith and I know that was a great comfort to him as he struggled with illness before his death.

In times of adversity, I have the great good fortune to have many wonderful friends around the country. In every corner of Ireland there are people who I can call friends. It is in those times of need that you really find out who your friends are. There are an awful lot of people I can turn to if I ever need support, including God.

In his 'Dark Sonnets' written in the face of intense despair, Gerard Manley Hopkins described his sense of being 'Pitched past pitch of grief'. I could not have articulated it as eloquently at the time, but I shared Hopkins' deep despair with my illness. In one of the darkest days in the history of my family, my mother's heart was smashed into tiny pieces overnight with my MS diagnosis and, years later, the same happened to me with my daughter Cora.

In the immense panorama of futility that follows a serious act of tragedy, our family, united in grief, struggled to comprehend the incomprehensible. With an inarticulacy born out of shock, sorrow and incomprehension – in what W.B. Yeats described in 'The Pity of Love' as 'a pity beyond all telling' – things which normally connected for a time no longer did. In the dark days that followed nothing connected with nothing.

One of the Latin phrases I heard in school was: *sunt lacrimae rerum*. Taken from Virgil, it means there are tears in the nature of things. The month of November – with All Souls – is the month the Church remembers all those whom we have lost. It indeed feels right and fitting that it should do so, as in the days, weeks and months of darkness after a bereavement, the wounds are often difficult to heal. It is painful for our shroud of suffering to be replaced by the translucent beauty of the Lord who rose from the tomb on Easter Sunday. We live through what Emily Dickinson refers to in her 'After Great

Pain' poem as 'The Hour of Lead' – a process of mourning that results in a final relinquishing, and an essential thaw.

Loss makes you re-evaluate what it is that matters to you. I did. I found the answer in my faith. The message of the Christian story leads us to accept disappointment and loss, but we never lose hope. Storms make the oak grow deeper roots. The rule of St Benedict, the ancient guide to the monastic life, includes the exhortation to 'keep death before one's eyes daily'. To some that may sound morbid, but to Christians in times of tragedy it is a reminder that we come into this world without fear and that our passing allows us to return without fear as well, crossing over knowing that union with God is our first and final home.

In November each year, the Church recognises that people are all the work of His hand, and that He is shaping us each day like the potter shapes the clay. This is so that we can begin to see that we are the work of the one who is the Life Giver and the Light Giver and begin to feel a new sense of our worth and value in life and death. Our loving God is the potter who will shape us to His image.


*My Other Mother*
The other person I give my allegiance to is Mary.

I like the idea of Mary as 'Our Lady of Health'. Every year in Lisbon they have a festival to her. This dates back to 1270 when the people of the city erected a statue to Mary, because Portugal had escaped the worst of the plague. In our age, where wellbeing is such a central part of the vernacular, perhaps there is something prophetic about the idea of 'Our Lady of Health'. Perhaps, though, it is even more important that we begin to rethink the way we understand Mary.

At the Annunciation, God asked Mary the question: 'Will you bring Christ into the world?' Mary's answer was yes. And gently Christ entered Mary, entered the world, entered our lives. For nine months, Mary was a living, walking tabernacle. Like us she asked, 'What is the meaning of God's presence in my life?'

Today we are faced with the same question as Mary: 'Will you bring Christ into the world?' Saying yes to that question means taking a real step in faith, because we do not know the full meaning of our yes. This will not unfold as we go along. But just as Mary felt the child grow within her and joyfully received Him on the day of His birth, so we will also discover that in our darkness, He is there – just as He has been all along.

These are often difficult times to speak about hope. Mary is traditionally presented as a woman of waiting and that gives rise to a problem in our culture where waiting is almost universally seen as something negative. There is a widely held belief, promoted very effectively by a whole range of marketing executives, that we can have whatever we want whenever we want it. So why on earth would you wait?

The Bible offers a different perspective and that makes it important for our time. It suggests that some things are worth waiting for and that the very act of waiting helps to nourish in us a sense of expectancy and of hope. The waiting that the Bible promotes is based on a trust that we will not be disappointed because what we are waiting on, hoping for and expecting, is nothing less than God.

The biblical texts invite us to take the time to reflect on what it is we are waiting for God to do. The people who assist us in this process are characters such as Isaiah, an old prophet; John the Baptist, a young prophet; and Mary, a pregnant teenager. Each in their turn is creative and imaginative, challenging and trusting, and they are all people of prayer. Isaiah dared to dream that deserts might be turned into fertile plains, that the blind might see and the deaf might hear. John the Baptist dared to challenge his contemporaries that they needed to think and behave differently if they wanted a better world and Mary of Nazareth dared to believe that God could act through her simple 'yes' to bring a light to the people who sat in darkness.

The reason we look to these heroes of hope and expectation is not that we are only interested in events of two millennia ago, but that we learn from them what to hope for and expect from God now, at this time in our world. We learn from them that when we make gods in our image and likeness, we will be disappointed. They teach us that the key is to let God be God and then transformation occurs. This, however, requires a prayerful waiting and that does not come easily to us in our instant age. But if we want our spirituality to mean something then we need to spend a little time with Isaiah, John and Mary.

Every day I try and let God be God.


*New Horizons*

My ministry continues to take me in ever new directions. I have collaborated with Orders like the Redemptorists and the Passionist Fathers for different occasions – including retreats. Sometimes this leads to moments of unexpected humour.

One day, while I was working with the Redemptorists, a fella came up to me and asked me earnestly to pray for him because he was looking for a woman! Before Christmas one year, a woman came up to me in a church because she wanted to confess her sins and said, 'Bless me, Father, for I have sinned.' When I tried to persuade her to confess to a priest she said back to me, 'Aren't you holier than any priest!'

I am particularly keen to nurture the faith of the next generation. As the late philosopher John O'Donohue said, we live in an era where we pay homage to image. And this is part of the reason that most young people do not know what it is like to share anymore.

I am fascinated by the sales every year. People stand shivering outside in the cold waiting to buy yet more 'stuff' they do not need. They remind me in a funny way of farmers I know outside Athlone who have three thousand acres, but if a half an acre came up they would be in for it like a shot. I know how much many young people love shopping, but it always amuses me when they spend hours shopping and come home with no new purchases. When I ask them why they bought nothing they always say: 'There was nothing in the shops.' Even so, we are indoctrinating our young people into the competitiveness creed, driving them on to a 'get out of my way' mentality. The drug in consumerism means that you can never be happy because its whole driving force is to get more and more and more and the more you get the more you want. This can come to the fore in the run-up to Christmas.

## The Eyes of a Child

People often say Christmas is too commercial, but I disagree. You only have to watch a child's face on Christmas morning and see that magic is more than just presents. I think children today are just as enraptured by the beauty and joy of the season as I was when I was a little girl. This is a time of mystery, magic, hope and above all innocence.

For me, Christmas is a time to slow down and take stock and be aware of the spiritual significance of the season. I am a committed member of the Church with deep faith and, for me, there is a joy in thinking of a child born in a stable who was sent to save people: the real meaning of the season is that God so loved the world that he sent his only son to save us.

I just love Christmas. I love everything about it – the tree, the holly, the exchange of gifts and going to the midnight Mass in my local church. But, above all, I love the spirit it creates every year when for a few days people are nice to each other. I even see it when I'm being driven in the car. Normally people won't give you the chance to get your car on to the main road, but for those magic days everyone is incredibly kind.

As someone who in recent years has experienced 'fake news' up close and personal, I am evangelistic about what constitutes the Good News. Of course the 25th of December is special because we also celebrate the greatest Christmas gift of all time. Little things do mean a lot. As we prepare for Christmas, we remember that God has showered us with gifts – none more so than when he sent his only Son.

The birth of Jesus offered a new beginning to the world, a new way of life. In this special season we are called again to take up Jesus's invitation to make a new beginning. The heart of this invitation is love because it is through love alone that we please God and our main challenge is to acquire such love. Jesus came on earth to love and be loved – to win love for our love. The Christian life is an exchange of love – the love we receive and the love we give God.

For all our society's claims to tolerance, pluralism and liberal values, the phrase 'born again Christian' continues to attract derisory remarks and condescending laughs. Someone who claims to be 'born again' is immediately written off as a way-out, eccentric category of Christian, at least in certain quarters. Yet I celebrate the term.

However, this new birth brings new responsibilities and

difficulties. The Bible can never be accused of misleading advertising because it portrays the Christian as someone who is active, tough, hard-working and dedicated. As we read in the Second Letter of St Paul to Timothy, there's the soldier who in war must be disciplined, obedient and courageous; the farmer who toils long hours and never has the luxury of a day off, and the athlete who pushes his body to the limit to maintain peak fitness and whose sights are fixed exclusively on winning the race.

Christmas is an ideal time to be reborn in Christ. This is not to take out some kind of salvation insurance policy, but to embrace a challenge of unconditional love that is terrifying in its demands. Christ is our saviour, certainly, but he is also Lord and, unless we accept him in both roles, we are not reborn and we don't receive him at all.

I see Christmas as a special time to spread the Good News of Christianity.


## Let Them Know It's Christmas

One of the key messages of Christmas, which I celebrate anew each year, is the belief that: The old is past, there is a new beginning.

Sometimes we fear to take a new step, to speak a new word. Change is all around us and our task is to build a better tomorrow. I am very keen on the symbolism of Christmas.

Another thing that fascinates me is that Christmas is a time of apparent contradictions. A king is born as a commoner. A birth signals the death of the old regime. Strength is clothed in weakness. Riches are disguised as poverty. Yet the real message of Christmas is very simple – 'God so loved the world that He sent His only son.'

The human capacity to take control of difficult situations is remarkable. In our complex world, to be in control is everything. Yet the paradox of Christianity is that the more we let go, the more we receive, because God's action becomes more effective in our lives.

God was born as a baby to highlight that in our weakness we will find strength to live the Christian life. If we were strong enough to do everything ourselves we would not have needed Jesus in the first place. Our earthly life is not a long examination paper where we earn salvation through our own feeble efforts but a chance to let God's love explode within us.

My wish at Christmas is that love will be all around.


*The Young Ones*

In April 2019 Pope Francis published an Apostolic Exhortation about the role of young people: *Christus Vivit* (Christ Lives). The document is based on a consultation between the Church and young people. Pope Francis honed in on the importance of young people in transforming the world when he said directly to them: 'God loves you and the Church needs you.'

This is a challenging task in an increasingly secular society. The difficulty is that the word 'Catholic' can have bad press in the twenty-first century thanks to catastrophic revelations in the recent past, with an ensuing overall lack of trust in the institutional Church. Even where such negative connotations are not immediately associated with any church-run groups, there can be expectations that whatever is Catholic is likely to be hidebound and conservative; fearful, guilt-ridden, puritanical and suspicious of success. For some in our society the very notion of 'Catholic' can conjure up images of sectarianism, of initiation to a cult, of some form of brainwashing to a particularly hard-line Catholic world view.

In marked contrast, Pope Francis states, 'An authentic faith – which is never comfortable or completely personal – always involves a deep desire to change the world, to transmit values, to leave this earth somehow better than we found it.'

We find God by reading the signs of the times. In an era when, for example, all students in a Catholic school can no longer be presumed to be from practising Catholic families, Pope Francis envisages with confidence a pluralist society in which current students will live and be the decision-makers and practise their own religious faith in peace and harmony with others.

Pope Francis follows the recent Synod of Bishops on *Young People, Faith and Vocational Discernment*, which outlines that: 'There have always been various forms of discipleship within the community of Jesus.' The Synod found that 'the young are called to make constant choices that give direction to their lives; they express the desire to be heard, recognised, and accompanied'.

Pope Francis is committed to developing ministry to young adults and to create opportunities for them to be accompanied on their journey of faith. He is exploring how this can best be facilitated in the light of the recent Synod which 'recognises the need to prepare consecrated persons and laypersons, male and female, who are qualified to accompany young people'.

The increasing lack of faith in the homes of young people is creating difficulties in primary schools in Ireland, particularly in areas such as sacramental preparation, as children prepare to receive Holy Communion. This has implications in terms of the relationships with God – if people do not know God themselves they cannot bring God to others.

Perhaps the crucial insight of Pope Francis in his *Christus Vivit* is to remind us all that God loves each one of us. I try to do my little bit to bring this message to others. I do some work with young people and I love it. One of the people I have helped out is Fr Patsy McDermott in St Mary's in Athlone. We have done retreats and other things with the youth. My philosophy is best summed up in the old Irish adage, *Mol an oige agus tiocfaidh siad* (Encourage the young and they will flourish).

In the media today, all the bad things in our world are highlighted, but we hear a lot less about all the good things that people are doing to help others. To take one example, just before Christmas 2017, over four hundred current and former inter-county football, hurling and camogie players joined forces to raise money and awareness for the homeless. The group, Gaelic Voices for Change, held a solidarity sleep-out in thirteen locations around the country from six p.m. to six a.m. They had hoped to raise €120,000 for charities north and south of the border, as well as to draw attention to the homelessness crisis. They ended up raising much more. Those involved believe that the GAA is based on community values and want to use their profile and their voices to support the vulnerable members in society.

As well as in towns and cities in Ireland, there were sleep-outs in Boston, New York and one former player even did it alone in Quebec, Canada. The then Dublin hurling manager, Pat Gilroy, joined his squad in the capital while the Clare hurling team joined the Limerick event.

The impetus for the response to the homelessness crisis was that Gaelic Games are built on communities, with a collective sense of belonging and supporting your neighbour. The sleep-out was a wider expression of that ethos by the players involved, extending a helping hand to others in our community. Prominent former players involved included Valerie Mulcahy, Diarmuid Lyng and Eamon Fennell. David Brady spoke movingly about why he got involved.

In the run-up to the event, he was in the city centre of Dublin. A man shouted across at him and the former Mayo star went across to speak with him. The homeless man was from his hometown in Mayo and in that moment Brady understood the homelessness crisis in a real way for the first time.

We speak when we do not speak.

We act when we do not act.

Gaelic Voices for Change showed us that we do not have to simply curse the darkness. We can light a candle when it comes to the homelessness crisis and all of the pressing problems facing us today.

Athlone's most famous man today is the great Irish rugby player Robbie Henshaw. With his sisters Ali, Emily and other family members, Robbie used their great musical talents to make a wonderful fundraising CD, *The Secret Sessions*, with the iconic Sharon Shannon for the South Westmeath Hospice. This is one of the many good things young people are doing today and they need to be encouraged to continue in that way.


## Serving the Lord

I have a carefully formulated strategy for working in the service of the Lord. I never felt I had to be a number one. Whenever I am asked to visit a church, I always make a point of kneeling before the priest to make a public statement of the importance of the priest. Keeping obedience to my bishop and priests is important to me.

My clarity about the role of the priest is complemented by a very clear philosophy of my own position. I'm me and I don't change. Other people, though, see me in a different light. Whenever I'm with someone I try to let them know that they are the most important people to me.

Most times when I am asked to visit a church I give a testimony. After all these years what surprises me is that there are some people who still come to hear me again and again. I asked one woman why she kept coming back and she said: 'No matter how often I come I get something new from it.' Even Jimmy says he always gets caught up in the story although he's heard it so often before. He told me that when he's watching me giving a talk he's thinking, 'That's the woman I married. Where is she getting all this wisdom from?'

I stepped back a few years ago from my public role because I felt that some people were trying to put me up on a pedestal and I thought to myself: 'I'm not a nun. I've got a great marriage, lovely children and grandchildren. I am a wife and a mother and I'm not going to let that go away from me.' It is important for me to have that balance. The ministry takes up an awful lot of my life, but I still want to have as normal a life as much as possible. I'm comfortable with myself and that's very important.

People sometimes say half seriously to me that I must be making millions from all these visits. I have never once asked for money to speak anywhere or to visit someone who was sick. I have got as payment for such speaking engagements various gifts such as plants and flowers. Probably the payment that stands out the most was a half-pound of rashers!

## A Pilgrim's Progress

Pilgrimages have always been an integral part of my apostolate. I bring groups to Fatima and Medjugorje. I have developed a good working relationship with Marian Pilgrimages down the years. They are very professional and good to deal with from my perspective.

I don't believe in shoving religion down people's throats. When

I go on a pilgrimage I have three rules. No one pushes religion on anybody. Nobody asks anybody their business. And, thirdly, I don't mind them having a drink as long as they know when to come home. The pilgrims always call me 'Mammy' because I'm always one step ahead.

There are times when it is challenging. Once I had two sisters who were sharing a room together and they started fighting like cats and dogs. It was getting to a stage where it was really having a negative impact on the group. I prayed for guidance, so then I asked one of them if she would mind if I put her beside someone I was worried about. She said, 'No. I'm staying with my sister.' I then asked her sister if she would fill in instead and she replied, 'No. I'm staying with my sister.' All of a sudden they were best friends again. Problem solved.

It was on a trip to Medjugorje that I launched one of my most cherished projects.

There were prayer groups to Our Lady of Lourdes and Our Lady of Fatima, but there was nothing to Our Lady of Knock. While I was away with my friends Mel McGuire and Terry White in Medjugorje I asked them if they were a member of any prayer group. When they told me they weren't I said, 'Well, ye are now.' So we began the first Our Lady of Knock prayer group. Once every month they meet in St Gabriel's Convent, Togher Road on the northside of Dublin. I devised a simple format for them and from time to time I visit them just to encourage them. Other such prayer groups have shot up in places like Roscommon, Cork and Mayo.

In recent years, the institution of the Church has changed a lot. When we were growing up in the country we found God in the fields, so we weren't dependent on the institution of the Church. Now that the institution of the Church has crumbled to some degree, the people are more aware that they are the Church and God is within us all. I think we are going back now to a Church that is made up of a lot of small groups.

We also have more praise. At first it takes a bit of a time to get into praise, but when you think about it it's not God that needs our praise it is we who need to praise God because it liberates us. On some level, when we praise God – or somebody else – it liberates something precious inside of us.


## On the Outside Looking In

My story continues to attract ongoing media and public attention. I have been featured on *Channel Nine* in Australia; *Dateline* in America and on Michael Aspel's programme *Strange But True*, where Mary McEvoy, Biddy from *Glenroe*, played me.

While my story is increasingly known I have never lost the ability to surprise the media.

A journalist from a national newspaper came to interview me a few years ago. She told me afterwards that I wasn't what she was expecting. She said, 'I was expecting somebody very pious, but you're a very ordinary person. Yet when you start talking there's a different person there even though you are still the same person. I was expecting someone who was wealthy but you just live in small house. I came here to tear you apart but I just can't find any reason to do that. You didn't give me any ammunition.'

A number of years ago, when Pat Kenny was presenting, I was invited to be on a panel for *The Late Late Show*. I declined initially because I was due to be speaking early to the next morning in the Graan in Enniskillen at an event that Fr Brian D'Arcy organised. Fr Brian was always good to me. The researcher told me that, 'Fr Brian would understand.' I told her that it wasn't just about Fr Brian, it was because I did not want to let down all the people who would be travelling to the event. They found a compromise by getting a car to take me there early the next morning.

One of the guests on *The Late Late Show* that night was Jeffrey Archer. When we were in the green room afterwards, his new book was there on a table but I didn't have my glasses so I was reading through it sideways. I was taken aback when Jeffrey Archer came up to me and said, 'That's the first time I've seen anyone reading my book sideways.'

I said to him, 'This is Ireland. We do things differently here.'

Very early the next morning the car brought me up to Enniskillen. When he was introducing me, Fr Brian said, 'I've always wanted to say this but finally now I can. Directly from *The Late Late Show*, please welcome Marion Carroll!'

## Help Me if You Can

It is not the media that keeps me going. It is the comments of the people I meet through my ministry.

It is not always wonderful. Somebody once described me as 'a well-paid actress'.

I have to confess that this remark really hurt me.

There are, though, so many people who are incredibly supportive and affirming. Just to pick a few examples. I could give hundreds. Once I went on one of my regular visits to the North of Ireland and I was approached to visit the son of a Protestant minister who was very unwell. I brought a picture of Our Lady and blessed him and he made a perfect recovery.

Another time I was invited to speak in Kilnacrott in County Cavan. I have no idea what came over me but I was in the middle of my testimony when I suddenly got this sense and I heard myself saying, 'There is a person in the room who is really afraid. If you stay with the crowd we will save you.' After the meeting was finished and everyone had left, this young man came up and told me that he was the one I was talking about. He asked me, 'How did you know?' I answered, 'I don't know.' To be honest I still have no idea how I knew. I cannot go into the details, but suffice to say he was on the run from some 'bad men'. We were able to get him to safety.

Another time I was in Galway and I met a young lad who was in a bad way. I bought him a cup of tea and gave him my phone number. Whenever I was in Galway I would meet up with him and gradually he started to get his life together. Then one time he came to visit me in Athlone and he was like a new man compared to the young guy in turmoil I had met a few years earlier. He told me that he was going to America to make a new life for himself. I was thrilled to see him looking so well, but he took me by surprise when he said that he had a gift for me. He added, 'I want to give you the book of my life.' Then he handed me a notebook. I flicked through it and I said, 'Thanks so much, but I don't understand. This is empty.' He looked me straight in the eye and said, 'If you hadn't come along this is exactly what my life would have been.'

I would not swap moments like those for all the money in the world. Of course it is nice to hear someone like the late Bishop of Elphin, Christy Jones, say, 'In a world filled with bad news, Marion Carroll's story gives hope and inspiration to us all.'

### The Circles of Friendship

Another great blessing in my life is the friendships that I have made throughout my ministry. I have known some very dark days and, like everyone else, I have knocks and setbacks which make me doubt myself. At times like that, apart from my family, the one group who has consistently sustained me and encouraged me when I was feeling down or frustrated has been the stewards and handmaids in Knock. They have been a rock for me, particularly in my hard times.

I would need a separate book to thank everyone who has been a friend to me. People like Teresa Farrell and her family have always been there for me whenever my spirits needed a boost and I will always be grateful to them for that reason. Vincent Grimes and his family have been a tower of strength also. I could not ask for better friends than them.

Sometimes my friendships and ministry are intertwined. An example that will illustrate is the great friendship I have developed with Kathleen Kelly. A year or so after my cure I was up in Tyrone and Kathleen was introduced to me because of some health issues in her family. We 'clicked' and she asked me to speak and pray with some of her friends. As the relationship developed she started to invite me to visit her in her home in Trillick. Initially I gave my testimony to some of her friends and people who had heard about me. The people come to see me on the basis of word of mouth.

However, over time the process has changed. I now go up to visit her three or four times a year. Kathleen has a room with an altar and a statue of Our Lady and I start in there at nine a.m. and I finish up around five p.m. I talk and pray with the people who come and there is a constant stream of visitors all day. It is always a great privilege when people share their stories with you.

Through my friendship with Kathleen I had one of my most intense experiences. One of her family friends was thirty-six weeks pregnant. She had a stroke and her husband came home and found her lying on the floor. She was rushed to hospital in Belfast. The baby was delivered safely, but the mother was in a critical state. Kathleen's family contacted me and asked me to go and pray with her in the hospital. I got the train from Athlone to Belfast and I prayed with her. The lady had tubes down her throat and as I was leaving she pointed to them, indicating to the medical staff that she wanted them removed and that her recovery had commenced. After the baby was born a member of the medical staff had pinned a photo of the new child on the wall beside the mother and she also pointed at the photo to show that she wanted to see her baby. I am not claiming the credit for her recovery, but it was incredibly exhilarating to see this up close and personal.

It shows that you should never lose hope.

This is a lesson I have learned well since my illness.

It is also a reminder that we can have tales of the unexpected. I have my own experience with those also.


*Graceland*

I always had a secret dream.

I have always loved Elvis Presley. My one dream was to get into Elvis Presley's bedroom.

I did!

There were serious breaches of protocol required and, to protect the anonymity of the guilty parties, the details of how it happened have to be preserved as if it was the fourth secret of Fatima! It is a long story, but I was over in America as part of my ministry and in the best Irish tradition I knew someone who knew someone.

I met a lady who was very, very taken by my best testimony and wanted to do something very nice for me. I told her what my one dream was as a laugh, expecting her to laugh back at me, but amazingly she put a series of measures in place and I was whisked into Graceland under the cover of darkness. I was given an access-all-areas pass! I had no interest in seeing Priscilla's bedroom or Lisa Marie's bedroom. I had only eyes for Elvis's bedroom. It did not disappoint. It was stunning with a big red carpet. All his cloaks and belts were there. He obviously had a very reflective side because there was an ornament representing good and evil. The rest of the house was very impressive also, particularly his den. What struck me the most was he had a big statue of the Sacred Heart.

I was told that I was the first woman to be in Elvis's bedroom. Years later Oprah Winfrey did a television programme on location in Graceland and she was boasting that she was the first woman to be in Elvis's bedroom. If she only knew it was actually a woman from a small house in Athlone!

Dare I say it, pun intended, it was a moment of grace for me.

### The Transfiguration

In recent years Jimmy has diabetes and is not always able to travel with me, especially when the grandchildren need looking after. He comes as often as he can and says he can see the change whenever I stand up on an altar or visit the sick. I'm still the same, but there is a transfiguration.

The transfiguration of Our Lord had always fascinated me but I never really could understand it. Then one day as I was giving my testimony in Falcarragh, just like the whispery breeze that came to me in Knock, the transfiguration was something I myself experienced.

Fr Pat Glennon from St Mary's in Athlone asked me once to give a reflection on the feast of the Transfiguration of Our Lord. Before I spoke that day I had no idea what I was going to say. In these situations I pray and I stand up and I'm never afraid. The Lord gives me the wisdom and knowledge I need for whatever situation I find myself in. On that occasion when I got up it all came to me. In the Bible, the past was Elijah. My past was my illness. Then, in the Gospel, God came down on earth in his son, Jesus – with whom he was well pleased. The day that I was cured in Knock was the day God let me know he loved me. Finally the Holy Spirit came to me when I saw my own heart.

I have reflected long and hard about my own apostolate. The Lord has given me a gift. I can talk to someone about death and dying and let them know the Lord will bring them home and protect them. I can empathise with them because I have been so close to dying myself. For the seventeen years when I was sick I was in the world but out of the world. When people see the sick they see the physical, but they don't know what it is like. There is an emptiness, a black hole that you can't share. I can't even share it with Jimmy because it is outside his own experience. It's a very lonely process.

They also tell me things that they can't share with others. When they talk to me I tell them, 'It's you, me and the Lord.' I have taken a vow of confidentiality not to repeat what is told to me. Whatever happens when people approach me for help I stay with them wherever their journey takes them – whether it be to recovery or home with the Lord. It is a big responsibility because when the Lord gives you something like this you really have the world on your shoulders.

## Don't Forget to Remember

When God is ready to call me to my final reward how would I like to be remembered?

For me, there is one thing that is crucial: love. I would like to be remembered as someone who gave God's love to others. My own experience of God's love is impossible to describe. If I could paint I could draw it or if I could compose I would put it to music, but I simply can't put it in words.

My favourite reading is from Chapter 13 of St Paul's letter to the Corinthians:

> 'Love is always patient and kind; love is never jealous; love is not boastful or conceited; it is never rude and never seeks its own advantage, it does not take offence or store up grievances. Love does not rejoice at wrongdoing, but finds its joy in the truth. It is always ready to make allowances, to trust, to hope and to endure whatever comes. Love never comes to an end.'

Love is unending because love is undying.

# 14

# From Darkness to Light

*'The best thing about the future is*
*that it comes one day at a time.'*

— ABRAHAM LINCOLN

I hope that when God calls me to the Pearly Gates I can stand tall knowing that I have made my small contribution to the advancement of society. I have done so without fanfare but in a quiet way, often hidden from the eyes of the world. But activities, such as those which cause the child to grow in the womb, do not have to be dramatic to be extremely effective.

There is no need to preach your virtues if you live by them.

Across the infinity between the living and the dead I wish my story to be an incarnation of messages of hope and new beginnings. And I wish to thank all of those who have helped me on this, my journey.

In practical terms I could not have navigated the journey without the support of Niall Glynn and all the wonderful staff at Marian Pilgrimages Ireland; Mairead and Jimmy Peoples and all the staff at the Drummond Hotel in Ballykelly, Derry, and Brian Crowley and all the staff in the Knock House Hotel.

What I hope is that my story can offer people an image of the new life that God is bringing in a way that could fill their hearts with hope for the future of the world, a belief that there was the possibility of a very different way of living. I hope in my small way I can help others to begin to hope and trust that it could happen, not just in the promised eternity, but that a beginning could be made in their specific context. With hope in their hearts, and a vision to inspire them, I believe that they might begin to play their part in bringing God's vision about.

I am enthralled by the compassion of God and Jesus to people. I am always inspired by the image of Jesus in the Gospels. He was someone who brought the compassion of God to people, someone who did not judge or condemn. He was someone who was with people wherever they were, especially those who found themselves on the margins of society. That is why I never fell prey to defeatism.

Love of God was expressed not only in prayer and Sunday worship for Jesus's fledgling community, but permeated every aspect of their lives. His world, like ours, desperately needed to be taught compassion in society and in religious communities – especially where there was and continue to be marginalised and rejected people. He exhorted his flock to seek to spread peace and harmony.

In the Gospels, Jesus clearly displays his closeness to the marginalised, such as lepers, prostitutes and tax collectors. Jesus introduces Himself as the person in whom was fulfilled God's promise to send one who would come to bring good news to the poor, to proclaim liberty to captives. Central to his teaching was the proclamation that the poor, the suffering and the hungry are blessed by God. These were passages that spoke to me.

His message was in stark contrast to many religious leaders who were stressing the need to live a good life so that people could save their souls and get to heaven and preserve themselves from the jaws of hell. In contrast, Jesus highlighted that God was working away in their lives, and that they do not see Him, because His plan is different. Accordingly, the attitude that needed to be developed was one of openness to Jesus, of trying to learn His way. Just as it happened to Mary during her pregnancy, God would grow in the lives of Christians through the ordinary living of their lives. Jesus wanted his followers to reach for the light for a new and fuller existence and to discern 'the Truth's superb surprise' – as articulated in Emily Dickinson's memorable phrase ('Poem 1263') – and to identify the key principles on which to build a better future. In many ways, Jesus was ahead of his time both in his approach to the individual in society and the uniqueness of the individual.

In contemporary parlance, Jesus wanted his followers to 'walk the talk' in their dealings with others. He wanted his followers to live the Good News rather than feebly mutter it.

Jesus's message resonates within our own lives and speaks to our restless hearts: words of wisdom that echo down the years and reveal a man of deep spirituality, fully human and fully alive, who never lost the common touch. His words hold a universal truth and remind us that all things pass, and the ultimate, unchanging truth is found within the heart's depths, a world of beauty and wonder, waiting to be explored.

Each of us are unique manifestations of the love of God. Self-esteem is seeing ourselves as God sees us. I want to share God's love.

I have never doubted that a small group of committed people with ideas and vision can change the world. Why? It is the only thing that ever has.

I love the story of a child who is on the beach and picks up a starfish and throws it back into the sea.

A man comes along and asks him: 'There are thousands of starfish on the beach. What difference do you think you are making?'

The child answers: 'I am making a difference to that starfish.'

I do not have the power to change the world.
But I can make a difference.
I am going to try to.

# Afterword by John Scally

I grew up almost as a neighbour to Marion. Although I do not live in the town of Athlone, I grew up close by in Curraghboy. Athlone was always part of my address. Both of us grew up in a time and place where we were encouraged, mostly indirectly, to keep our heads down. When Marion first spoke to me about working with her on her book I did not hesitate for a second because I felt it was long overdue that people like her get the chance to tell their story.

I applaud her for having the courage to put pen to paper.

After captaining America to a tense victory at the Belfry in the 1993 Ryder Cup, Tom Watson quoted from Teddy Roosevelt, words that I would readily agree with:

'It's not the critic that counts, not the one who points out how the strong man stumbled or how the doer of deeds might have done them better. The credit belongs to the man who is actually in the arena; whose face is marred with sweat and dust and blood; who strives valiantly; who errs and comes short again and again; who knows the great enthusiasms, the great devotions and spends himself in a worthy cause and who, if he fails, at least fails while bearing greatly so that his place shall never be with those cold and timid souls who know neither victory nor defeat.'

I am grateful for all Marion's help in writing this book. Hers is the idealism of youth and there is not the slightest trace of cynicism or disillusionment, though there are hints of a steely resolve behind the mild, almost innocent exterior. To spend time in her company is a pleasure and a privilege. She is a woman of sharp intelligence, good humour, passion, a tornado of energy, and a shotgun blast of opinions. She also has an uncanny ability to hold up the mirror to Irish society and her mind is as sharp as an executioner's axe. To listen to her talking was an education because of her penetrating scrutiny of issues.

My thanks also to Jimmy. George Eliot's comment on Dorothea Brooke in *Middlemarch* could apply to Jimmy:

'But the effect of her being on those around her was incalculably diffusive: for the growing good of the world is partly dependent on unhistoric acts; and that things are not so ill with you and me as they might have been, is half owing to the number who lived faithfully a hidden life, and rest in unvisited tombs.'

Very particular thanks to Niall Glynn and all the wonderful staff at Marian Pilgrimages Ireland for their support of Marion over many years and especially for supporting the book launch.

Special thanks to Mairead and Jimmy Peoples and all the staff at the Drummond Hotel in Ballykelly, Derry for their consistent support down the years.

My most profound gratitude to Brian Crowley and all the staff in the Knock House Hotel who have been unwavering in their assistance to Marion for many years.

My thanks, too, to Bishop Francis Duffy for permission to quote from his homily at Knock and likewise to Archbishop Michael Neary for his permission to quote from his homily.

I remember with affection two great champions of Marion: Monsignor Joseph Quinn and Bishop Christy Jones.

I am grateful to Kathleen Kelly, Pat Lavelle, John Hynes and Brian D'Arcy for sharing their insights with me.

Marion's grandchildren have all been great to her, but I have appreciated Chantel's technical assistance in this project.

I am very thankful to James Wims for his help with photos.

As always I am grateful to my good friend John Littleton for his practical assistance with this book.

Thanks to all at Black & White Publishing, particularly Campbell Brown for backing this book so enthusiastically. My thanks also to Simon Hess for his support.

John Scally
January, 2020